OUR FIGHT FOR AMERICA

Also by Michael Savage
published by Center Street:

Stop Mass Hysteria

Trump's War

God, Faith, and Reason

Teddy and Me

Scorched Earth

Government Zero

Stop the Coming Civil War

OUR FIGHT FOR AMERICA

The War Continues

MICHAEL SAVAGE

CENTER
STREET®

NEW YORK   NASHVILLE

Copyright © 2020 by Michael Savage

Cover copyright © 2020 by Hachette Book Group, Inc.

Hachette Book Group supports the right to free expression and the value of copyright. The purpose of copyright is to encourage writers and artists to produce the creative works that enrich our culture.

The scanning, uploading, and distribution of this book without permission is a theft of the author's intellectual property. If you would like permission to use material from the book (other than for review purposes), please contact permissions@hbgusa.com. Thank you for your support of the author's rights.

Center Street
Hachette Book Group
1290 Avenue of the Americas, New York, NY 10104
centerstreet.com
twitter.com/centerstreet

First Edition: September 2020

Center Street is a division of Hachette Book Group, Inc. The Center Street name and logo are trademarks of Hachette Book Group, Inc.

The publisher is not responsible for websites (or their content) that are not owned by the publisher.

The Hachette Speakers Bureau provides a wide range of authors for speaking events. To find out more, go to www.HachetteSpeakersBureau.com or call (866) 376-6591.

Print book interior design by Timothy Shaner, NightandDayDesign.biz

Library of Congress Cataloging-in-Publication Data has been applied for.

ISBNs: 978-1-5460-5949-3 (hardcover), 978-1-5460-5967-7 (large type), 978-1-5460-5948-6 (ebook)

Printed in the United States of America

LSC-C

10 9 8 7 6 5 4 3 2 1

CONTENTS

OUR FIGHT FOR AMERICA

ONE

THE TWIN PLAGUES:
COVIDISM AND COMMUNISM

This book is not about a man. It's about a nation. It's about a fight that can't be fought by one man. It must be fought by all of us. I have been on the radio for over twenty-six years spreading the news and doing my part to resist the radical left's war on our borders, language, and culture. Over the past year, they've escalated it to a nuclear war, figuratively speaking. Every news story has become a dirty bomb; every American institution a target. But, of course, the two things exploited most by the left so far have been the coronavirus and the murder of George Floyd.

Yes, I'm calling it murder because that's what I saw when the police officer so charged knelt on a handcuffed, defenseless man for over eight minutes.[1] There was good reason for outrage. A black man had been arrested for allegedly passing a counterfeit twenty-dollar bill. After watching the heartbreaking video, I said the officer should have been charged with first-degree murder and a hate crime. I still stand by that. But I condemn the way the left exploited this tragedy for political purposes.

The killing of George Floyd arrived in a perfect storm. The country had been locked down and crippled for three months. People were pent up. The students were not in school. That's when the left struck. Cities were looted and burned in an unprecedented orgy of organized violence.

President Trump showed tremendous restraint in not calling out the military, which had been done to quell riots many times before. Meanwhile, the liberal governors in New York, Illinois, Minnesota, Michigan, California, and other blue states, who had imprisoned their populations well beyond any plausible medical necessity and destroyed the economies of their states based on fraudulent and misinterpreted data, had nothing to say when tens of thousands of left-wing rioters socially embraced to burn and loot.

Suddenly there was no talk of masks, of social distancing or washing your hands. No, there was only talk of revolution from the mouths of these governors. But don't be confused. This is nothing like the American Revolution that won our independence from Great Britain. This is more akin to Mao Zedong's Cultural Revolution, the ten-year reign of terror he visited upon the Chinese people to wipe out the last vestiges of capitalism and the traditional Chinese culture and impose his own brand of communism, called Maoism.

If you think that's hyperbole, think again. One of the many wonderful tactics of Mao's Cultural Revolution was public humiliation. In what were called "struggle sessions," people suspected of being enemies of the communist state would be set upon by coworkers, friends, or relatives and subject to verbal and physical abuse. Students were often pitted against their teachers, friends against friends, even spouse against spouse. If the person was important enough, the session might even be held in a stadium before tens of thousands of people. Victims were often physically tortured.[2]

Well, that wonderful communist practice has come to America. During the riots in May and early June, a Massachusetts police chief lay facedown on the ground for over eight minutes with his hands behind his back as if he were handcuffed during a Black Lives Matter demonstration. I'm not sure if it is better or worse that this self-humiliation was done voluntarily. What I do know is this type of thing will cease to be voluntary if these subversives get their way. I also know trying to appease this mob is not going to help. The crowd may have been yelling, "Thank, you, Chief!" while he performed this self-deprecation, but at least one bystander remarked, "It's not enough, but it's a start!"[3]

Nothing will be enough to satisfy these people. That's because they are not primarily civil rights activists. They just use that as a wedge. They are primarily Marxists who want to tear down and rebuild our entire society. Don't take my word for it. Just read the Black Lives Matters (BLM) website. They're quite open about what they want.

> We disrupt the Western-prescribed nuclear family structure requirement by supporting each other as extended families and "villages" that collectively care for one another, especially our children, to the degree that mothers, parents, and children are comfortable.[4]

I hope I don't need to tell you that every communist since Plato has wanted to break up the nuclear family and have "the village" raise the children. But it isn't just this disturbing passage on their website that otherwise somewhat obscures the communist principles of this group. Take a look at who founded the organization. The bio on Opal Tometi's TED Talk web page says, "She is a student of liberation theology and her practice is in the tradition of Ella Baker, informed by Stuart Hall, bell hooks and black Feminist thinkers."[5] Baker, hooks, and Hall were all well-known Marxists, Hall having founded the *New Left Review*.[6] BLM cofounder Patrisse Khan-Cullors sits on the board of the Ella Baker Center for Human Rights and their third cofounder, Alicia Garza, is special project director for the National Domestic Workers Alliance.[7]

Saying policing in America began as "slave patrol," Tometi suggested that police departments should be eliminated and the officers who currently protect us from violent street gangs, murderers, and rapists be replaced with social workers.[8] And, of course, a lot more of our money. Tony Williams, a contributor to another left-wing group called "MPD150" (signifying the 150 years the Minneapolis Police Department has existed), told NPR that we wouldn't need police if we just use "public health approaches and getting people resources to meet people's needs. Crime stems from inequality, and if we can take care of each other we won't need police."[9]

I'm not sure if this is a cynical attempt to leave Americans even more at the mercy of the violent street gangs, both homegrown and those pouring over our southern border, or just the most acute case of that mental disorder called liberalism I've ever seen. So, when there is a bank robbery or a home invasion, they're going to send in social workers? Lots of luck with that, liberals. Of course, this will all be after we've been fleeced for even more of our money to provide the "resources to meet people's needs." It's always one more handout that will solve all of society's problems—until it doesn't. Then, it's another and another and another.

So, no, this is not about the wrongful killing of a black man, which I, myself, wholeheartedly condemn. This is about much more. This militant, communist group, Black Lives Matter, has gone mainstream, with the left-wing multinational corporations trumpeting their brand. They previously led the movement to abolish the Immigration and Customs Enforcement (ICE)[10] and now want to abolish police departments. It won't stop there. They will eventually call for abolishing the nuclear family, capitalism, private property, and the rest of our way of life.

This is what we're up against. Covid-19 was a real public health threat and George Floyd's killing was a genuine wrongful killing by a police officer, possibly even a hate crime. But the reaction to both has been pure opportunism by the left to destroy what is left of our capitalist economy and our borders, language, and culture, just as Mao Zedong tried to do in China. They must be stopped and *we* must stop them. By "we," I mean anyone who doesn't share their vision of a cultureless, borderless, socialist slave camp run by liberal bureaucrats and "woke" multinational corporations. This is *our* fight for America.

THE CORONA CATASTROPHE

History teaches us one undeniable reality: every great civilization eventually ends. Whether mighty empires like Rome or Spain, federations like the Dutch Republic, or great Italian city-states like Florence, Milan, Venice, and Genoa, they all had their dominant period and all eventually fell or declined into minor powers, relegated to the pages of history for future great civilizations to study. In many cases, epidemics played a major role in their demise.

Will Covid-19 similarly play a role in our own? It's too early to tell. This nation has been through serious epidemics before, some far deadlier than this, but never one that has had nearly the widespread effect. While this virus will pass, nothing about America is ever going to be the same again. As I've said since I started my radio career, a civilization is defined by its borders, language, and culture. What of this nation's borders, language, and culture will survive?

In my many decades on this planet, I have seen a lot of changes. I remember the 1960s, when twentieth-century America was forever changed, for the better in some ways and for the worse in others. I remember Martin Luther King Jr.'s famous speech and heroic African Americans marching peacefully to victory in the struggle for civil rights. But I also remember the beginning of bum culture in Haight-Ashbury, the strung-out hippies who had "dropped out" of society to take drugs and litter the streets with their squalor.

I remember when the Berlin Wall fell in the late 1980s and, a few years later, the entire Soviet empire. The Cold War I had lived with my entire life was gone in what seemed like an instant. The "evil empire," as Ronald Reagan called it, had once placed nuclear missiles ninety miles off our coast in Cuba and the whole world held its breath, wondering if there would be a world to wake up to the next day. Thirty years later it was gone.

I've seen it all or I thought I had, until earlier this year, when the coronavirus first hit our shores. Never have I seen a society implode the way America did under not just the threat posed by the virus, but the government reaction to it. Governors called upon arcane emergency powers laws to shut America down in a way no one would have thought possible even one year ago. And Americans obsequiously obeyed. Let's face it, we gave up our liberty without so much as a whimper. My long-standing motto has been "borders, language, culture." Where was American culture when these draconian measures were taken? Where was the rugged individualism, the defiance? Two hundred forty-five years ago, Patrick Henry thundered, "Give me liberty or give me death!" In 2020, Americans said, "Give me Netflix and take-out. That's good enough for me."

The conservative movement as we knew it is dead. President Trump bailed out everyone and don't think for a moment the bailouts are over, even now. Had "democratic social-ist" Bernie Sanders won the presidency he could never have achieved what occurred while capitalist Donald Trump was president as far as moving this nation toward socialism is con-cerned. We are a socialist nation at this point. I can give you six trillion reasons why and counting.

Now, you can say the president was backed into a cor-ner, with no realistic options other than those he chose. His early instincts that something was wrong with locking down the entire country were politically untenable, largely because there was no one around him giving him sound public health advice. Did he ever even hear the words "selective quarantine" from anyone from the CDC or NIH? I think we all know the answer to that. All he had was Anthony Fauci and Deborah Birx, "Dr. Slouchy and the Scarf," as I call them, telling him martial law was his only option.

You could also say that he never wanted to spend six trillion dollars bailing out everything from the Kennedy Center to gargantuan restaurant chains like Ruth's Chris Steakhouse while the little guy, the small, independent, family-owned restaurants, got nothing.[11] I know several owners of such restaurants personally in my home city of San Francisco whose establishments barely survived or didn't survive. They didn't get any help from the government, but J. Alexander's Holdings, which owns 46 restaurants in 16 different states and did $247,269,000 in net sales last year, got over $15 million.

That's how government bailouts have always worked. The banks get bailed out first. Next are the corporate leeches who can afford an army of lobbyists. And when that feeding frenzy is over, whatever scraps are left are thrown to the unconnected, while the cameras roll to aggrandize the politicians. You can say Trump had no choice but to allow all that or the little guys would not even have received what they did. But it doesn't change the result: socialism has arrived.

Yes, I still support President Trump, but we need to support him with our eyes open. I don't expect him to deliver 100 percent of what I or like-minded people want. No politician can. But we can't blindly cheer his every move, rationalize away the socialism or the lack of a border wall four years after he was elected. Oh yeah, the wall. Remember that? Or has this coronavirus erased your memory, too, along with so many others'? It hasn't erased mine. And the facts are that more people are pouring over our southern border than ever before. California even sent them their own bailout because they supposedly didn't get stimulus money.[12]

I warned you about the "true believers" in my previous book, *Trump's War*. Well, that warning has turned out to be prescient. Blindly supporting everything the president does and rationalizing away every misstep or failure does him no service. It does America no service. It's my job as an independent member of the media to be a thorn in the side of the government, even when it's being run by someone I support. It's your job to allow criticism when its warranted without becoming a quasi-religious fanatic, questioning nothing your leader does and howling at those who do, like those we so rightly criticized when Obama was in power.

Economically, the New Gilded Age is over. That's not a terrible thing. There were excesses that could not go on forever, fueled by fraudulent fiat currency irresponsibly created by the Federal Reserve. There was wanton destruction of the natural world, of forests, the seas, and our furry and finned friends. Nature, as she always does, made a correction. Does that mean we need the insane Green New Deal? Of course not. That's more about social and economic control than it is about saving the earth.

As I've said so many times on my show, there is a middle ground—the Dao, if you're familiar with Eastern philosophy. I've been saying for years that conservatives must reclaim the concept of conservation from the far left. They've allowed the maniac socialists to completely commandeer the idea of stewardship of the earth we inhabit. That must change if America and the rest of Western civilization is to get off its back and survive.

Part of whatever replaces the conservative movement in opposition to the socialists must include the distinctly conservative concept of conservation. Conservation and environmentalism are two different things. Environmentalism is closer to a pagan religion, worshipping the earth and nature as an entity to be defended against the evil human race, especially the lighter-skinned part of it. Conservation recognizes man as part of nature, the highest, most enlightened part. Man is supposed to be a steward of the natural world of which he is a part.

This is not a left-wing concept. Certainly, you must have noticed that "conservative" and "conservation" come from the same root word. Both are derived from the Latin, "conservare." Conservatives used to understand that their ideology was based upon conserving not just long-standing sociopolitical norms but conserving the natural world. The first American conservationist president was Teddy Roosevelt, a Republican. Somehow, that concept got lost amid the yammering of uneducated talk show hosts that defined the conservative movement in its dying days.

THE END OF GLOBALIST "CAPITALISM"

So, too, will end unrestricted free trade. That's not wholly good or wholly bad. Long before Donald Trump stormed the Republican Party and its globalist mantras, I was pointing out that there is more to life, individually and as a nation, than getting consumer goods at the absolute lowest price possible, all other considerations be damned.

Has international trade conferred benefits on Americans? Certainly. Has it raised millions in Third World nations out of extreme poverty? Absolutely.[13] But at what cost? And who has borne the cost?

I think you know the answer to that. One of the main problems with these so-called free trade arrangements is they have been largely one-sided. The premise of all of them was that it was the United States' responsibility to allow all the wretched, socialist backwaters of the world to "catch up" by being able to export their goods freely to the United States while maintaining trade barriers against U.S. exports. China is only the largest, most glaring example. But China is instructive. It has only done to a larger degree what dozens of other countries have done: rise to relative prosperity on the backs of American workers and taxpayers.

If you think it's only electronics and other consumer goods that are no longer manufactured in America, you've got another thing coming. Back in February, I had Rosemary Gibson as a guest on my radio show, *The Savage Nation*. Gibson is the award-winning author of a number of books on the medical industry and is considered a national authority on health care reform. Her new book, *China Rx: Exposing the Risks of America's Dependence on China for Medicine,* confirmed a lot of my worst fears about the effects on our domestic supply capabilities of medicines and medical supplies.

It's not the final drug that China necessarily controls, but the key ingredients needed to make the final product. China may control as much as 90 percent of that market. Gibson spent three years researching her book and came to the conclusion that "in the event of a natural disaster or a global pandemic, the United States will stand in line behind other countries" for the ingredients it needs to make lifesaving drugs.

This is a significant risk that past administrations hid from you. Allowing China to accumulate this much power over the supply of medicines could prove disastrous for the United States should China decide to cut off that supply. Paranoid? Don't kid yourself. They've already floated the idea through their state-run media.[14] I would recommend against allaying this concern simply because China didn't play this card during the first wave of this epidemic. If the past twenty years have taught us anything, it's that China is willing to play the long game while narcissistic U.S. politicians set their sites on plundering the rest of us in two- and four-year increments.

Well, one disaster may have come along to wake us up to the threat of another. Covid-19 is going to end economic globalism as we have known it these past twenty to thirty years. We're going to be bringing production back home for a lot of things, including vital medicines. What has been called "free trade" will no longer nullify all other considerations. Fear of foreign-born diseases may do what losing our manufacturing capabilities couldn't do: make Americans reprioritize.

It is not as if China hasn't been damaged by this pandemic. It now has a credibility problem all over the world, thanks to its early dishonesty about the coronavirus and ongoing suppression of knowledge. And it's not as if they were winning before this. Donald Trump had finally done what so many sellouts before him had failed to do. He stood up to them. It wasn't as if they were going to win, as long as America tried. Representative republics with market economies will beat authoritarian state socialism every time, as long as the former doesn't intentionally let the latter win.

Who is going to be eager to use Chinese imports after this? Who won't be worried they aren't sending another disease in their containers full of cheap crap? America won't drop imports from China cold turkey, but a major reset will occur. That goes for all global trade arrangements. An era of relative isolationism is coming, for better or worse.

International trade has been spreading epidemics for thousands of years. The Roman and Han Empires were self-sufficient in all their essential commodity needs. Foreign trade for these ancient peoples was largely for luxury items, which were marginal to their everyday needs.

Even in ancient times, foreign trade contributed to cultural interchange and to the spread of the great world religions, especially Christianity and, later, Islam. Trade was the conduit through which was created what used to be called "Christendom."

However, there were other, less fortunate consequences of the world trade routes, including the spread of disease. The Plague of Athens in 430–427 B.C. is one example. It killed nearly a third of the Athenian population and resulted in the Athenians burying their dead in mass graves.[15] This happened during the Peloponnesian Wars and may also have been the result of overcrowding within the walls of the city and poor hygiene.

The Antonine Plague of A.D. 165 was another related to war. It broke out first among the Huns, who infected the

Germans. The Germans spread it to the Roman army, which brought the disease home and spread it throughout the population. Symptoms included fever, sore throat, diarrhea, and pus-filled sores. It may have been an early incidence of smallpox. Marcus Aurelius himself died of the disease.[16]

Of course, the most infamous epidemic in human history was the "Black Death," a bubonic plague epidemic that killed 30 to 60 percent of Europe's population between A.D. 1347 and 1351 That disease also originated in China and spread into central Asia via the Silk Road trade route, where it eventually spread into Europe, also via international trade.

Several Italian city-states had trade relationships with Asia. The Genoese in particular had a colony at Kaffa on the Crimean peninsula by permission of the Mongols. When that relationship deteriorated, the Mongols laid siege to the city. In 1346, the plague hit the Mongol troops besieging Kaffa, who by some accounts catapulted the bodies of those who died from the plague into the city. That story may not be true, but we do know Genoese merchants eventually brought the disease to Italy.[17]

Epidemics fall into two main groups: smallpox or measles and bubonic plague. Studying the historical accounts of epidemics leaves no doubt that they had devastating effects on vulnerable populations. Of the arrival of smallpox in China in 317, Chinese historian Ssu-ma Kuang wrote that "one or two out of a hundred survived."[18] So, the death rate wasn't two percent. The death rate was *ninety-eight percent.* Was he accurate? We can't be certain, but it's clear he means an awful lot of them died.

WHY HAVE A NATION?

The economic and political damage done to our country by the Corona Catastrophe and the carefully cultivated communist riots, under the guise of civil rights, is extensive, but there is something more fundamentally important that has also changed: our culture. The America we knew and loved is never coming back. I hate to be the bearer of bad news, but it's my job to tell you the truth, not necessarily what you want to hear. We have to face life in a new America and try to make something livable out of it. Right now, it is not livable.

Think about what we did last spring. Do you think it's not all coming back? What reason do we have to believe that shutting our society down won't be the new normal in the face of any threat, real or imagined? Had we put up any semblance of resistance to the insane edicts of Democrat governors, then maybe a chance for sanity would have survived. But we didn't. We rolled over and hid under our beds, the young and healthy alike with the old and infirm. Don't think that didn't send a message to every power-mad politician in this country, of which there are many.

Just think about Americans going about their lives in masks for most or all of the year. We all look like bank robbers or surgery interns, all these hysterical Americans wearing masks while bicycling or running in the park. Madness! We no longer treat each other the same way we used to. People don't embrace when they meet anymore. They don't shake hands. Personally, I've never been a hand shaker myself, being a germaphobe, but most Americans were. Not anymore. The summer came and our restaurants continued to go out of business because they weren't allowed to seat to capacity. Large summer events were canceled in advance because preparations for large events begin months in advance and America was shut down when the organizers needed to be preparing them.

America was a nation of independently owned restaurants, bars, and cafes. We rivaled Italy in that respect. That's over, too. Those independent establishments that survived the first shutdown won't survive the next. The big chains will be just fine on billions in bailout money. That's convenient, isn't it? So, prepare to trade in that favorite little corner pub or family-owned Italian restaurant for Applebee's or the Olive Garden. I'll pass.

What about large sporting events, the movies, the theater, or the opera? All these activities had one defining feature: sitting in proximity to your fellow Americans. Let's face it, the seats at the baseball game had you practically sitting in your neighbor's lap. Again, that's not my cup of tea but it was an integral part of American culture that's also gone with the corona wind.

I have news for you. It's not just Trump that has a war on his hands this time. It's all of us. We are at war to preserve our nation, our Constitution, and some semblance of our humanity. As I said in an earlier book, *Trickle Down Tyranny*, "Economies can be rebuilt, armies can be repopulated, but once a nation's pride is gone it can almost never be restored." We're going to need something much stronger than the quaint old conservative movement to regain our freedom and independence. This virus, the many left-wing riots, and our collective reaction to them was an invitation to all the enemies of both. The socialists, the technocrats, the globalists, and the Deep State have seized the opportunity this crisis has presented them. They have nonstop propaganda support from the media. This is what we're up against in our fight for America.

TWO

THE VIRUS PROFITEERS

The Corona Catastrophe is a disaster for our nation, our economy, our freedom, and our culture. But it's not a catastrophe for everyone. No, there are some people for whom this is the best thing that ever happened. Just as the 9/11/2001 attacks were exploited by the Deep State, giving them license to trample the Fourth and Fifth Amendments, track our emails, phone calls, and financial transactions, and run roughshod over our liberty, so, too, is this virus a Christmas gift to a rogue's gallery of tyrants, busybodies, and thieves.

If you want to figure out who benefits most from this disaster, simply precede the first sentence of this chapter with a question. *Cui bono?* That's Latin for "who benefits?" Who stands to gain from the destruction of our economy, freedom, and culture? Simple: every anti-American interest group we've been fighting for most of our lives.

THE DEMOCRATS

I suppose I should start by saying what I've said a hundred times on my radio show and will say again in this book. No, Covid-19 was not a hoax perpetrated by the Democrats to harm Donald Trump politically. I never said that and am not saying it now. In fact, I'm going to talk about the irresponsibility of even some normally reliable media on the right in suggesting anything of the sort.

Rather, Covid-19 was an opportunity that presented itself to the Democrats, much like 9/11/2001 was an opportunity for the Deep State to get everything they ever wanted. Do you think all three hundred pages of the Patriot Act were written in less than two months after the attack? Of course not. It was a hodgepodge of invasions into our privacy proposed or drafted over many years prior to 9/11. That's how things like this work. What is unthinkable at any other time suddenly becomes reasonable in an emergency, when the public is in a state of fear.

Look at spending alone. Were it not for the emergency, would Pelosi have been able to get $75 million each for the Corporation for Public Broadcasting, National Endowment of the Arts, and National Endowment for the Humanities, $88 million for the Peace Corps, and $30 *billion* for the Department of Education into one bill and have it passed 96–0 by a Republican-controlled Senate?[1] Of course not. Yes, there were plenty of Republican boondoggles packed into the bill, too. But that doesn't diminish what the Democrats were able to accomplish.

Profligate spending was only the tip of the iceberg in terms of the benefits this catastrophe conferred on the Democrats. They were headed for a landslide defeat in November with the Trump juggernaut rolling toward a showdown with a dementia-addled candidate who wasn't very impressive even when he had all his marbles. But a recession changes all that. Incumbent presidents generally don't get reelected during recessions and this virus has allowed state governments to bring one about, with Democrat governors leading the charge. Recession? They've caused a second Great Depression.

The Democrats are rejoicing in the suffering it has caused. They were already rooting for a recession long before the coronavirus. Speaking to an audience of investors in San Francisco in the summer of 2019, Trump economic advisor Stephen Moore said he didn't see a recession coming in 2020, adding the economy would soar if a China trade deal were accomplished. "I want a recession so we can get rid of Trump," responded one deranged member of the audience.[2]

Moore tried to reason with the lunatic, saying that even if you don't like Trump, you shouldn't root against America. While I agree with Moore in spirit, his response is everything that's wrong with the conservative movement. It's always bringing a knife to a gunfight with these anarchists. Don't root against America? That's what their whole movement is based upon. These people have been working to destroy everything about America that makes it America for over a hundred years. They are playing the long game and they don't take prisoners. You can't reason with them. They're not interested in considering another viewpoint. They don't want to meet you halfway or even consider meeting you some of the way. They have one goal: destroy what pillars remain of this once-free republic and impose a far-left, multicultural socialist framework on a center-right population.

You might wonder how a radical minority could accomplish such a feat in a supposed democracy. Well, let me give you a little lesson in how democracy really works. This is what they didn't teach you in public school, even back when high schools taught civics.

The first rule is majorities don't win elections. That's number one. Almost 40 percent of eligible voters don't vote in presidential elections[3] and almost 50 percent don't vote in midterms. Now, just take those facts and apply a little simple math. If only 60 percent of eligible voters vote in the presidential election and those are roughly split in half between the two candidates (not counting millions of illegal aliens and dead people voting for the Democrat), what does that mean? It means about 30 percent of eligible voters elect the president. Applying the same reasoning means about 25 percent of the population elects the representatives and senators elected during midterms.

Does this knife cut both ways? Sure, it does. You could say a minority of eligible voters elected Donald Trump. But then think about what those two, active minorities want. One wants to destroy the existing political structure and the culture that created it and replace it with something radically different. The other wants to *conserve* the political structure and the culture that created it. Now, which of those two movements is the apathetic group who don't vote more likely to align with?

Yes, you can criticize nonvoters all you want, but you can't escape the obvious. Those who are passionate to radically change the political structure are much more likely to vote. Those who are fine with the way things are, even if naïve in thinking they can take it for granted, are more likely not to vote.

Yes, Donald Trump's election was a revolution of sorts, but it was a change in direction, not structure. The left had managed to institutionalize some of its agenda in the decades that preceded Trump, but the real threat was the direction they were taking the country under Barack Obama and the acceleration with which their plans were proceeding. There were cracks in the foundation of our free society, fissures in some cases, but it was still intact. That was thanks to we in the minority who believed it was worth everything we had to preserve it.

Well, I'm not sure the foundation is there anymore. What evidence do you see that it is? So, if Lesson One was democracy doesn't result in the will of the majority, at least in the real world, then Lesson Two is the Democrats aren't interested in even the textbook definition of democracy. As I've said practically my whole career in one way or another, they're crypto-fascists. They are interested in absolute rule, no matter what percentage of the population agrees with them.

So, yes, they were glad to see the best economy of our lifetimes turn into a depression during an election year. The insane communist Alexandria Occasional Cortex was dumb enough to state this publicly. When oil futures crashed so hard they actually went negative, she couldn't contain herself. In a since-deleted tweet, she wrote,

> You absolutely love to see it.
> This along with record low interest rates means it's the right time for a worker-led, mass investment in green infrastructure to save our planet. *cough*[4]

"Worker-led." This is straight Marxism, right out of the pages of *The Communist Manifesto*. Or, you could say out of the policy manuals of Lenin, Stalin, or Mao, the policies that led to over a hundred million deaths in the twentieth century, not counting those who died on battlefields. We are already a socialist nation as of this past March. The next step would be full-on communism and a return to the mass starvation and totalitarianism that accompanied it during the previous century. Like each of those communist regimes, the one ushered in by Occasional Cortex or a like-minded tyrant features a nonsensical, top-down, central economic plan to override every aspect of the market economy.

THE ENVIRONAZIS

That brings us to the second group who benefit from this government-inflicted depression: the environazis. Yes, there is a lot of overlap between "Democrats" and so-called environmentalists, but the hard-left faction of the environmental movement doesn't include every Democrat. And the hard-left environazis couldn't be happier than they are now with a crippled economy, businesses working at half capacity or less, travel restricted, and bureaucrats ascendant.

Now, most well-adjusted people understood the Covid-19 lockdowns as catastrophic, even if some thought they were necessary. But not the environazis. The lockdowns are how they want us to live *all the time*. In fact, they want life to be even worse than it was during March through May of this past year. They don't even want the few people liberal governors in all their wisdom deemed "essential" to be working the way they do today. If they had their way, nobody would be flying, driving to work, or congregating in tall buildings in our centers of commerce.

There was a great book by Michael Crichton called *State of Fear,* which I'd encourage you to read if you have the chance. It's a fictional story, but it is bursting with truth about the false global warming narrative and its insane proponents.

One character is an actor named Ted Bradley, a typical Hollywood woodenhead who thinks he knows what he's talking about because he gets paid to recite someone else's words into a camera. At one point, he hauls forth with this.

> "Don't you think," Bradley said, "that's because it's the white man, not the natives, who wants to conquer nature, to beat it into submission?"
>
> "No, I don't think that."
>
> "I do," Bradley said. "I find that people who live closer to the earth, in their villages, surrounded by nature, that those people have a natural ecological sense and a feeling for the fitness of it all."

Doesn't that sound like the typical Hollywood liberal who lives in a mansion, gets to the airport in a chauffeured limousine, and then boards a private jet to fly to his next anti-carbon cult rally? Bradley romanticizes primitive people who live without electricity, motor vehicles, or machinery. This fixation with our savage past goes all the way back to the first modern socialist, Jean-Jacques Rousseau, who imagined primitive man as a "noble savage," at peace with himself and nature and incapable of deliberately injuring his fellow man because of his blissful ignorance.

Bradley eventually gets a fatal dose of reality about the true nature of primitive village life when his group is captured by cannibals and Bradley becomes course number one of a village feast. Unfortunately, the nonsense he peddles in the novel is alive and well all over the environmentalist left. They genuinely want to reduce us to primitive life, without air travel, automobiles, electricity, and heavy machinery. The lockdowns were only a glimpse of the destruction they would like to visit upon our civilization in the mad quest to heal their deity.

Of course, none of this would apply to them. No, they have work too important to be hampered by the inconvenience of public transportation or efficient housing. They have movies to make about the evils of businessmen and the "white supremacists" of their liberal fever dreams. They have taxes to redistribute to millions of illegal immigrants marching over our borders in caravans organized and funded by the Soros gang. It's everyone else who must sacrifice the benefits of the modern society they themselves built so Nancy Pelosi and Ben Affleck can bring whatever Somalis aren't already here over from Africa to make "Little Mogadishu" encompass all of Minnesota.

Mark my words, the environazis will not let this crisis go to waste. They're going to fight with everything they have against the economy ever coming all the way back. The only way they'll relent is if huge concessions are made to their Green New Deal agenda, including forcing us to pay through the nose for "renewable" energy and rebuild our houses and office buildings to meet their "sustainability" standards. The latter initiative will visit destruction on the economy that will make the economic damage done by all previous government edicts combined look like an accounting error.

MEDICARE FOR ALL

Speaking of economic destruction, have you noticed there are fewer hospitals and urgent care centers around? The Covid-19 lockdowns were supposedly imposed to protect the hospitals, to keep them from being overwhelmed by too many patients at once. Do you remember them telling you that? Well, that certainly begs at least one question: Why did the lockdowns stay in place when it was apparent not only that the hospitals weren't going to be overwhelmed, but that new infections were actually declining?

According to the city government's own website, New York City's cases and hospitalizations both peaked on April 6, after which they precipitously declined. The number of deaths peaked on April 7 and declined dramatically after that date.[5] Does that sound anything like the story you were told through April? Why did Governor Cuomo extend the lockdown in his state on April 16,[6] when it was clear based on the number of hospitalizations and deaths that the crisis was over?

At no time in March or April were New York City hospitals ever any more overwhelmed than they had been in previous severe flu seasons. The USS *Comfort* saw twenty patients its first day. It left New York City at the end of April having treated only 179 patients the whole time it was there.[7] The hospital tents in Central Park that liberal media breathlessly reported only had capacity for sixty-eight patients. As late as April 9 they still weren't at full capacity and as far as I can determine they never had more than fifty-two patients at any one time.[8] The media stopped reporting on them after that, most likely because there was nothing to report.

Not only was it never the case that hospitals in New York City—or anywhere else for that matter—were overwhelmed, but they were underwhelmed. Having canceled elective surgeries and other profitable work to make room for the flood of patients they were told was coming, hospitals were actually laying off and furloughing staff during the supposed crisis![9] Rural hospitals were especially harmed economically as they sacrificed their more lucrative business for Covid-19 patients, who for the most part never materialized.[10] As I've said many times over the course of this fiasco, epidemics are mainly an issue in densely populated urban centers. Covid-19 was no different. There was never a reason to lock down rural counties that weren't going to have large numbers of hospitalizations and there certainly wasn't a reason for rural hospitals to commit economic suicide, especially at a time when many rural hospitals were already closing.[11]

According to an analysis by consulting firm Guidehouse, 354 of the 1,430 rural hospitals in the country were already at high risk of closing before the Corona Catastrophe. And no, that doesn't prove the free market doesn't work for medicine. We haven't had anything like a free market in health care for a long time. According to NPR, "health experts" say a hospital's ability to survive the Corona Catastrophe may depend upon whether it is in a state that expanded Medicaid or not.[12] Those that did not are receiving lower federal reimbursements.

What does that tell you? Everything we predicted about Obamacare was correct. First, they're punishing any state that didn't comply by lowering federal reimbursements, which would mainly be Medicare payments. Did I not tell you one of the costs of Obamacare's health care handouts would be cuts to Medicare? In other words, they're expanding a program for people with no skin in the game at the expense of one where at least the recipients are required to contribute.

Plus, it shows how quickly Obamacare has deteriorated the strength of the health care system. It's only been fully implemented for six years and already hospitals cannot survive without it. Now, you add the lockdowns and, "Presto!" you have thirty million more unemployed people, most of whom will also end up on Medicaid. Once you get to a critical mass of people fully dependent on the government, the next step to "single payer" will not just be easier, it will be presented as the only way to avoid complete catastrophe. What seemed extremely unlikely before this lockdown hoax will instead seem hard to avoid. You may even see some Republicans supporting some transition toward more government health care.

Six months ago, Americans, even many Democrats, were breathing a sigh of relief that Bernie Sanders did not win the nomination. Well, they may have popped the cork off the champagne bottle a little too early on that one. Sanders won't be sitting in the Oval Office, but his policies will be. Single-payer health care was a major pillar of his socialist system and it's a lot more likely since the Corona Catastrophe.

THE ANTI-CASH CROWD

I've been talking about the government war on cash for many years. This is a global war, waged by the elites against cash transactions in every major country. Governments say they want to ban cash transactions because they help criminals. And yes, drug deals, illegal gun running, and other nefarious transactions are conducted in cash. But that's not the only transactions they want to track. They want to be able to track all financial transactions, including yours and mine. That way they can make sure they are squeezing every drop of tax money out of the citizenry. Every tip for a waiter or waitress, every dollar made from a garage sale. They even want a piece of your child's lemonade stand—if the child has the required permit.[13]

Cash represents financial privacy for more than just avoiding excessive taxes. The government really has no business reviewing any of your transactions, cash or electronic, unless they have probable cause you've committed a crime. While we can't trust them to obey that fundamental principle of freedom, we must at least reserve the right to transact in a medium they can't track.

The other major reason they want to ban cash transactions is inflation. By "inflation," I don't mean the phenomenon of rising prices, but the real definition of inflation, which is expansion of the money supply. Central banks in other countries are already imposing negative interest rates through inflation of their currencies.[14] That means savers are forced to pay borrowers for the privilege of lending them money. This insanity is the endgame of the so-called New World Order's fraudulent monetary system. Inflation is already a wealth transfer scheme from the majority of society to the financial sector. Once negative interest rates are in place, the rip-off increases by an order of magnitude.

Just as with government snooping, cash provides a refuge from this larceny. When all else fails, you can always pull your money out of the bank in cash and store it in a private safe or under the mattress. Negative interest rates can't touch physical cash stored privately. So, that's reason number two the parasite class wants to make cash illegal. That isn't a theory. It's been discussed openly in recent years.[15]

This will be easier, too, thanks to Covid-19. With irrational fear at an all-time high thanks to the governments' overhyping the danger of the coronavirus, businesses are already banning cash transactions themselves. "Payment is something that creates a lot of touch points for both the guests and our employees," said an assistant manager at a Sacramento restaurant. "To solve those problems, we went strictly to touchless payment."[16]

That doesn't seem all that unreasonable at the height of a pandemic, but don't think for a moment the government won't take advantage of the situation. Government-run Amtrak was quick to ban cash payments and we'll see if that policy is ever reversed.[17] The World Health Organization (WHO) was quick to take advantage of fear of the coronavirus by telling people it might be spread through currency.[18] For some reason, they felt the need to walk their comments back somewhat a week later after the original report went viral.[19] But the damage was done. Retracting their statement was a little like the news story that reports a man railroaded by an overzealous prosecutor turned out to be innocent. Nobody pays attention to the retraction. They just remember the guy was "in some kind of trouble."

So, be prepared for a full-court press to get rid of cash in order to make financial transactions "safer." They will be safer without cash—for government snoops and banksters. For the rest of us, banning cash will be just another way for the elites to loot our freedom and wealth.

BIG PHARMA

I probably don't have to bother to tell you that this pandemic and what the federal and state governments have chosen to make of it is one giant Christmas gift to Big Pharma. Forget all the usual corruption that goes on under the incompetent rule of the Food and Drug Administration. At least under normal circumstances, the FDA's crony drug manufacturers must put up their own money to develop their overpriced new drugs. Thanks to the coronavirus hysteria, they won't even do that.

The federal government has already handed out over $2 billion in grant money to four different firms just so they can try to develop a vaccine for Covid-19.[20] Over half of this money goes to a multinational corporation called AstraZeneca, headquartered in Cambridge, England. A half billion each went to Johnson & Johnson and Moderna, respectively. So, in keeping with the rest of the government response to this pandemic, it will be socialism as far as the costs are concerned, but capitalism when it's time to divvy up the profits. That is, unless the market crashes again, in which case it will be socialism for the losses.

President Trump's new "vaccine czar," as I call him, Moncef Slaoui, was a board member of Moderna when the president asked him to lead "Operation Warp Speed," the sadly accurate name of the federal government initiative to develop a Covid-19 vaccine. Now, see if you can follow this bouncing ball. Slaoui is asked to lead the project on Wednesday,

May 13.[21] According to CNN, he doesn't step down as a board member of Moderna until after the appointment.[22] On Monday, May 18, just five days later, the company announces "promising early results" for a potential Covid-19 vaccine, sending its stock up 25 percent that day.[23]

Now, Slaoui may have stepped down from the board before that, but he still owned millions in Moderna stock options. So, Slaoui stood to make a huge windfall off the price movement of the stock. I don't know if it made the difference or not, but I was calling attention to this conflict of interest loudly to my millions of listeners on *The Savage Nation* that entire day. By the end of the day, Slaoui had announced he would donate the proceeds from the windfall to cancer research.[24] Was that his plan all along? I don't know. I don't read minds. But if it doesn't smell a little fishy to you, see an ear, nose, and throat specialist.

Others who benefited from the news, which was vastly overstated, by the way—the trial consisted of only eight participants—didn't feel the need to walk away from their own windfalls. Two executives at Moderna sold almost $30 million in stock while it was up that day, making almost $25 million in profits, before the stock fell when experts weighed in to cast doubt on how good the news really was.[25]

See how that works? The federal government hands out your money to fund vaccine research by a private company, then lets insiders keep the profits made off pump-and-dump schemes based on bogus news about the vaccine being developed on your dime.

It was the same story with the development of remdesivir, a drug developed as a treatment for the coronavirus.

Three different federal agencies provided tens of millions in research support to help Gilead Sciences develop the drug but asserted no patent rights over the product.[26] So, again, your tax money provides capital for a private company to develop the product, but the corporation keeps all the profits.

This is only the beginning. Just wait until a vaccine or drug treatments are approved by the FDA. Then you'll really see the pigs gorging themselves at the trough. You can bet there will be calls for the vaccine to be mandatory, by both interested parties and useful idiots. Never mind that no effective coronavirus vaccine has been developed before. Even the flu vaccine is only about 50 percent effective on average, which is why I never take it.

It won't matter after the mass hysteria they've created over this coronavirus. There will be a full-court press to make it mandatory. Even if not technically mandated by law, the federal and state governments may make it so onerous to refuse the vaccine that it is mandatory in all but name—with the lucky drug company laughing all the way to the bank.

THE BIG MULTINATIONAL CORPORATIONS

The drug companies aren't the only multinational corporations that will benefit from the Corona Catastrophe. All our beloved "woke" corporations stand to gain from everything small businesses lose because of being forcibly closed down by the insane left-wing dictators running the states.

Independent and family-owned businesses are the backbone of America. They create most new jobs and are the stuff of our cities and towns. Every dollar earned by a small business is a dollar the large multinational corporations would like to have but haven't been able to outcompete the small businesses to get. There are some things Americans prefer to buy from small businesses, either out of loyalty or because small businesses just plain deliver a better product.

No matter. The state and federal governments are taking that choice away from you with a combination of lockdowns and onerous reopen regulations for small businesses and trillion-dollar bailouts for their giant multinational corporate competitors. The small businesses go under and the big corporations gobble up the unserved market share, using your money as capital.

An early estimate by the local Los Angeles CBS affiliate predicted 7.5 million small businesses were in danger of closing due to the coronavirus pandemic.[27] Actually, that report was misleading, whether intentionally or not. The pandemic wasn't what was putting the businesses in danger of closing; it was the government response to the pandemic, which we now know was grossly disproportionate at best and completely wrongheaded at worst, that endangered the businesses.

I also believe the estimate was too low, even though 7.5 million is about one-quarter of all small businesses in the country. That's because it's not just the months of lost revenues these businesses suffered under the lockdowns, but the impossible restrictions on their operations after the economies were "reopened." Anyone who has ever run a small business that makes sales in person knows you need to maximize revenue per square foot.

If you own a restaurant, that means tables relatively close together and every table full on your busiest nights. If it's a retail store, you need heavy foot traffic with people in every aisle on your busiest days. You also need to make the experience as pleasant as possible for people visiting your store. Exclusive men's clothing stores may offer you premium coffee or other amenities to augment the experience. It's difficult to bring in enough revenue to cover your overhead, much less distribute something to the owners. That's why so many restaurants and retail stores fail even under normal circumstances.

Well, under the guidelines imposed on them even after they are allowed to "reopen," it's practically impossible. For example, the executive order issued by the Lansing Lunatic, Governor Gretchen Whitmer of Michigan, requires retail stores, among other things, to "post signs at store entrance(s) instructing customers of their legal obligation to wear a face covering when inside the store, and install physical barriers at checkout or other service points that require interaction, including plexiglass barriers, tape markers, or tables, as appropriate, design spaces and store activities in a manner that encourages employees and customers to maintain six feet of distance from one another."[28]

I know Comrade Whitmer doesn't have to worry about this, but all these requirements cost money, something small businesses didn't have after being forcibly closed for two or more months. And they weren't even able to meet their monthly overhead, much less underwrite all this redesigning and remodeling, with the draconian limits on customers in their stores after they were permitted to open:

(1) For stores of less than 50,000 square feet of customer floor space, must limit the number of people in the store (including employees) to 25% of the total

occupancy limits established by the State Fire Marshal or a local fire marshal. Stores of more than 50,000 square feet must:

    (A) Limit the number of customers in the store at one time (excluding employees) to 4 people per 1,000 square feet of customer floor space.

    (B) Create at least two hours per week of dedicated shopping time for vulnerable populations, which for purposes of this order are people over 60, pregnant women, and those with chronic conditions like heart disease, diabetes, and lung disease.[29]

So, independently owned retailers will be permitted to open if they have the money to completely redesign and remodel their stores, but those few customers allowed inside at any one time must wear a mask, meaning they will buy what they came for as quickly as possible and get out. That means fewer, if any, incidental sales, another vital component of any small retailer's revenue.

What business could survive under these conditions? Answer: a business getting government money to subsidize their losses. But the mom-and-pop restaurants and retailers didn't get Paycheck Protection Act money. I know several small business owners who tried to get SBA-backed loans and couldn't. Not so for their multinational competitors. More than two hundred publicly traded companies got loans totaling more than $750 million.[30] Also at the receiving end of the gravy train were companies under federal investigation, with accounting problems, or with bad credit.

In some cases, this even goes for hospitals. Yes, many small, rural hospitals closed or will have to close because of the insane policies their governments enacted in response to the coronavirus. But for large, wealthy hospital chains like HCA Healthcare, it was just the opposite. Despite earning over $7 billion in profits over the past two years and paying their CEO $26 million in 2019, this conglomerate got over $1 billion in bailout money from the federal government.[31]

If that sounds like a bad joke, wait until you hear the punch line. After this company worth $36 billion received the bailout money, it still laid off or cut the pay of tens of thousands of doctors, nurses, and lower-paid workers.[32]

They aren't alone. Twenty of the largest hospital chains received over $5 billion in federal bailout money even though they collectively had cash reserves of over $100 billion. Providence Health System has $12 billion in cash reserves but still got $509 million in bailout money. Like many hospital groups, Providence is set up as a nonprofit organization, so it doesn't even pay federal income taxes. Meanwhile, smaller, poorer hospitals are receiving next to nothing.[33]

Whenever politicians start handing out money, a good portion of it inevitably goes to people with political connections. The PPP was no exception and the largesse was truly distributed in bipartisan fashion. Among the organizations that received money were political organizations run by both Republican Grover Norquist and Democrat Madeleine Albright, and a "political strategy firm linked to two alumni of the Obama White House."[34] Schools where both President Trump's and former President Obama's children are or have been enrolled also received funds.[35]

Funds also flowed to Kanye West's clothing line, the Girl Scouts, and many hedge funds.[36] A dozen or so tech startups and venture capital firms received loans.[37] Gay dating app Grindr and Burning Man, the drug fueled freak fest in the middle of the desert, got $1–2 million and $5 million, respectively. Somehow, we can do without independently owned hardware stores and restaurants but we can't do without them.

Americans were led to believe these funds were going to be made available to truly small businesses, like the independently owned grocery store in your neighborhood or the local dry cleaner. I'm not saying no funds flowed to businesses like that, but an awful lot seem to go to people who could have got by without them. We were also told the primary reason the program was created was to preserve the jobs that would otherwise be lost. Yet, a total of 48,922 guaranteed and potentially "forgivable" loans were provided to companies reporting "zero jobs retained." One company, Zilber LTD., got $7,500,000 for retaining zero jobs.[38]

You can download all the PPP loan data, including the over 660 thousand loans exceeding $150,000 at https://sba. app.box.com/s/tvb0v5i57oa8gc6b5dcm9cyw7y2ms6pp.

For many of the small businesses the CARES Act was supposedly written to help, even those that got loans didn't find them useful because of the strings attached to keeping the money.[39] For example, 75 percent of the money had to be spent on payroll, which means it couldn't be used to help with all the new costs that state and local governments put on businesses as a condition of reopening.

The Corona Catastrophe will disproportionately affect small businesses, many of which will not survive. Large multinational corporations, on the other hand, who can count on the Federal Reserve to bail them out with newly printed money even during normally occurring recessions, will not only survive. They will acquire all the market share previously held and lost by the little guys the government put out of business. And it will all be paid for by taxpayers, whether directly in new taxes or in the higher prices resulting from all the Federal Reserve monetary inflation.

Who else benefits from the Corona Catastrophe? This summary is by no means an exhaustive list. As time goes on, the list will grow, but you can count on one thing: all the forces that want to transform America from a prosperous, free, capitalist nation into a poor, authoritarian, socialist one will benefit from the government response to this virus. The forces of evil are relentless, and they truly never let a crisis go to waste.

THREE

WILL OUR BOLD PEASANTRY GO GENTLY INTO THAT GOOD NIGHT?

Ill fares the land, to hastening ills a prey,
Where wealth accumulates, and men decay:
Princes and lords may flourish, or may fade;
A breath can make them, as a breath has made;
But a bold peasantry, their country's pride,
When once destroyed, can never be supplied.

—OLIVER GOLDSMITH[1]

That was from "Deserted Village," written in 1770 by Oliver Goldsmith. Goldsmith was an Irish-born poet who was friends with some of the great literary and political luminaries of his time, including Samuel Johnson, James Boswell, Sir Joshua Reynolds, and Edmund Burke. For some reason, these words came to my mind during the psychopathic destruction of society by left-wing governors based on political motivation and fake data about a serious but not catastrophic epidemic. Maybe it was thuggish police beating up old men in line waiting to have pancakes with their elderly wives on Mother's Day because some fascist, left-wing governor told them to enforce social distancing laws beyond all reasonable limits.[2]

At the same time, farmers were killing pigs, cows, sheep, and goats, plowing under their crops, and spilling milk into creeks, ostensibly because there are no buyers for these products with most restaurants, hotels, and schools closed.[3] It killed me to watch the stupidity and the mismanagement of the federal government.

I have studied history. I know about the famines that led to Mao Zedong's communist revolution. I read about the famines that followed Stalin's misguided agricultural policies in the 1930s, resulting in death by starvation for thirty million Russians. Well, famine may follow this disaster because of the idiocy of the federal government. There is never an excuse to waste food on a scale like this. Have they never heard of freezing?

The Chinese do not slaughter their pigs and throw them into their rivers or burn their animals alive. They're smarter than we are, maybe from experience. They slaughter the animals they can't use and freeze them. The farmers don't do it; the government does. They actually auctioned off thousands of tons of pork from their frozen reserves to stabilize prices earlier in the year.[4] They're smarter than we are. It's better to bail out the farmers, saving crops and livestock for future use, than to bail out the hedge funds.

You can't eat a hedge fund, can you?

Then again, most "progressive" Americans are waiting for the billionaires to eat each other. They used to say, "eat the rich," but now they're hoping the rich will eat each other. They probably will, after they get done eating us.

A friend emailed me while all this was going on, distraught that I seemed to be one of the only other people to understand at the time. Shops, restaurants, and other businesses that depend on in-person sales cannot survive in the "new normal." How could this have come as a surprise to anyone? When you go into a restaurant on a Friday or Saturday night and it's not crowded, the first thing you think is, "Oh, they must be in trouble." Everyone knows restaurants must be crowded on their busy nights to survive. They can't afford to pay for non-revenue-producing square footage. Neither can department stores, shoe stores, or convenience stores.

The big players like J.Crew and Nieman Marcus went into Chapter 11 bankruptcy court, which simply means some creditors took a write-off, some management floated away on their golden parachutes, and the companies had an excuse to let go their more experienced, more expensive employees. New vultures took over to gobble up Federal Reserve monopoly money to leverage the companies to the hilt once again, buying back shares and putting absolutely nothing aside for a rainy day.

It's a much different story for the family-owned business renting space in a plaza with a personal guarantee for the lease. There is no golden parachute for those business owners. Once their governor puts them out of business, they lose not only their life's work but the house they put up as collateral for the lease. That family-owned Italian restaurant that still makes the same sauce your parents and grandparents used to love before you were even born? Forget it. They're gone. You'll have to settle for Olive Garden, owned by conglomerate Darden Inc., which had its hand out early for bailout funds when the federal government and Federal Reserve rang the dinner bell.[5]

The formerly proud owners of these quintessentially American small businesses will become managers for the large corporations to avoid starving to death. The idea of independent business ownership will largely be dead in America. This is just getting under way at the time of this writing. We've heard the bomb go off, seen the flash, but haven't yet seen the crumbling of the buildings and the devastation. That's partially because the government has artificially held everything up with bailouts based on printed money.

This is not without a cost. By early May, we had already seen the warning signs of price inflation, something a whole generation has grown up without having to worry about. Those of us who remember the 1970s know how devastating inflation can be to the middle class. Well, the cost of groceries rose the fastest they had in forty-six years shortly after the first wave of money printing by the Fed. The U.S. Labor Department reported on May 12 that the prices U.S. consumers paid for groceries rose 2.6 percent in one month, the largest month-over-month rise since 1974.[6]

This will be another nail in the coffin of our "bold peasantry." Of course, America doesn't have peasants. Goldsmith was writing before the industrial revolution created the vibrant middle class that defines America. Instead of peasants working small farms we have shopkeepers, restauranteurs, barbers, tradesmen, landscapers, and many more running small businesses. These are what comprise the infrastructure of every community in America. Sure, there are fast food chains, department stores owned by large multinational corporations, big-box retailers, and large grocery chains. I'm taking nothing away from any of them; they all have their purpose and part in making America what it is. But no one thinks of them when they think of their city or town. If someone asks you what you love about the place you live, do you ever say, "We have the best Nordstrom's"? Of course not.

When friends or relatives visit your town for the first time, you generally don't get excited to take them to the local Applebee's or Carrabba's. You want to show them the little corner Italian restaurant that's been owned by the same family for the past hundred years and still makes its own bread every day. You want to take them to that corner bar where the staff knows you and half the customers can walk home if they get too tipsy.

When you need a new light fixture hung or a pipe replaced, the guy who shows up to help you doesn't work for a company any hedge fund manager ever heard of. Often, he's a small business owner who employs three or four other people as helpers. If you don't cut your own lawn, it's a small business owner and his or her employees who take care of it for you. The little diner you stop into for bacon and eggs on Saturday morning, the barbershop or hair salon where you get your hair cut, and the ice cream stand you wait in line in front of on warm summer evenings are likely all family or independently owned businesses.

Do you have children learning to play a musical instrument or do you play one yourself? There's a good chance there is an independently owned music store in your neighborhood that sells instruments and gives lessons. The Walker Music and Textile Company in Hastings, Michigan, was just such an establishment until they were pronounced "non-essential" and ordered closed by the Lansing Lunatic governor Gretchen Whitmer. The local Fox news station interviewed the owner, who broke down in tears talking about his life's work being eliminated.

"It's not just the closing of a stupid store," he said while weeping openly. "It's the closing of a dream. It won't be a retail shop anymore and it won't be an inviting environment for kids to come and be loved and to learn music," he added.[7]

I can't remember when I've seen something so painful. He and his son sat in chairs playing guitars in his closed shop until the father could no longer continue. He had watched those businesses allowed to stay open to some degree scratch and claw to survive, but he wasn't even allowed to try. This is what happens when the government picks winners and losers. Who is any bureaucrat to say what is essential and what isn't? It's not as if they have ever provided a product or a service anyone bought voluntarily. These people have no idea what it takes to make payroll or come up with a new product line. They operate on precisely the opposite incentives. When they fail, their department or agency gets more money. When a business owner fails, he goes out of business.

Steve Walker hadn't failed. He was put out of business by a tyrannical government.

The same state government was after seventy-seven-year-old Michigan barber Karl Manke. He was also ordered to close down, an order he complied with until he couldn't afford to any longer. "I was denied twice for unemployment. I haven't seen anything in one these other checks from the government," he said.[8]

Of course Manke hadn't seen any federal bailout money. Only "woke" multinational corporations are eligible.

So, Manke opened his barbershop in defiance of his insane governor. The state tried to get a court order to shut him back down, but the judge they petitioned refused to grant the order without a hearing. Unwilling to be inconvenienced with something so trivial as due process, the state summarily suspended Manke's license.

Manke kept on cutting hair anyway. What a tough old bird. "The government is not my mother, never has been," he said after the license suspension. "I've been in business longer than they've been alive."[9]

That's an American patriot speaking. Where has that spirit gone? That's not to say there was no support. Manke worked forty-five hours during the first few days he was opened, according to local reporter Bria Jones, who went live through Facebook as people lined up to get their hair cut and drivers honked their horns in support.[10] A few days later, an armed militia arrived at his door to defend Manke from the police, if necessary.[11]

That's a foreboding development I'll have more to say on shortly. Manke is an outlier, one of those few who stand up when all the world around is running for cover. Too many like him are too afraid to dissent and it's hard to blame them. But more frightening still is the amount of people who are cheering on this destruction of our middle class. Are Democrat voters that insane that they want Amazon and Google to own everything, just because the companies are run by liberals? What happened to "small is beautiful"? What happened to "buy local" and all the other hippie mantras about supporting the little guy against powerful corporations?

These are our "bold peasantry" and just as Goldsmith said, once they're gone, they can never be replaced. This is the price we're paying for the devastation these left-wing dictators have visited upon our country. It's hard to believe they are not destroying this country on purpose. It's not just Cuomo in New York and Newsom here in California. Governor Gretchen Whitmer of Michigan has made quite a name for herself as an economic grim reaper. It wasn't just the order to close Manke's barbershop that had Michiganders taking to arms. More than once, armed protestors showed up at the capital to demand she rescind her insane lockdown orders, to no avail.

In what has become a trend among these totalitarians, she expressed utter contempt for those protesting, as if their petitions for redress were something she need not consider. Appearing on that bastion of liberal nuttery, *The View,* Whitmer said, "These protests, in a perverse way, make it likelier we're going to have to stay in a stay-home posture," Whitmer said.[12] Not only does she dismiss legitimate protests protected by the First Amendment, but she issues a thinly veiled threat: protest my edicts and you will be punished with extensions to the lockdown.

This isn't about public safety. It's about unwavering obedience to even the most ridiculous orders of an out-of-control
liberal governor. Of course, being a liberal, she felt compelled
to call the protestors racists.[13] What else can anyone who
doesn't suffer from the mental disorder called liberalism be
but a racist? Some of the protestors had swastikas or other
Nazi symbols, but they weren't carrying them to proclaim
themselves Nazis. They were telling her *she* was acting like
one! From her comments, it appears she realized this but tried
her best to mislead the gullible, of which there are tens of millions, that the protests themselves were motivated by racism.

It's the same old story, isn't it? She didn't use the word
but Whitmer was just rehashing Hillary Clinton's declaration
that the half of the country that didn't agree with her were "a
basket of deplorables." It wasn't even new when Clinton said
it. "The race card" is an expression only because liberals have
been playing it for so long it might as well be a pair of twos.
Calling conservatives racists is just their way of saying what
is in their minds and hearts: they hate our bold peasantry.
They hate everything these true patriots stand for, everything
they represent. They hate them because they are America, the
nation and the idea, which they want to erase from history.

WILL THE LOCKDOWNS IGNITE A SECOND CIVIL WAR?

We're on the cusp of a civil war. It has broken out in only a
few places so far and on a minor scale. One of the stories that
struck me early on was of the police officer in the Port of
Seattle. He was a former special forces operative who fought
in Afghanistan who was placed on paid leave after posting
a video online telling fellow police officers they should not

enforce unconstitutional coronavirus-related orders.[14] Officer Greg Anderson was thrown off the force because he believes in the U.S. Constitution. Fortunately, he's not alone. There are tens of thousands of police officers who agree with him, not to mention millions of Americans who would likely join a revolution right now to overthrow the tyranny we're living through. Here is something Anderson said on the almost nine-minute video that began his difficulties:

"I think what is going to happen, if this continues, is we're going to see bloodshed in the streets," said Anderson. "I don't want to see bloodshed in the streets on either side of this coin. I don't want to see fellow officers injured or killed and I certainly don't want to see citizens get injured or killed. You don't get to just say, 'Well, I'm doing this because I was told to do so,' or 'I'm following orders.' My personal choices and my living arrangements, no matter what they are, don't allow me to trample on people's rights."[15]

For refusing to enforce the communist dictates of his governor, this George Washington of our time was kicked off the police force. This is a man who fought on the streets of Iraq and said this destruction of our rights was going to "wake a sleeping giant," meaning the American people, who will "fight ten times harder for their freedom on their soil than anything you've ever seen before."

This isn't some millennial blowing off hot air in his mother's basement. This is a police officer who has been in combat, who has seen civil war firsthand, who would not tell people they weren't allowed to go to church. He refused to stop them to see "their papers." He understands what's at stake. Governor Newsom does not. Neither does Nancy Pelosi nor the creature governors in Colorado, Michigan, or many other states. They do not understand what we the people are capable of.

Around this time, I was pruning an old tree before going on the air. It was all tangled up in some bushes. I could still see leaves growing on the highest branches. On the bottom, most of the branches were dead. They had been that way quite a while; it's an old tree.

So, I got out a saw and started to cut away the dead wood. I had to be very careful to make sure there were no leaves growing at the top of the branches I was cutting, which I assumed were completely dead. I got a certain satisfaction as I cut off the dead branches of this old tree to let the new branches live. It was like I was cutting away tyranny to let the tree live free.

While doing so, I thought of people like Nancy Pelosi and our Democrat governor, Gavin Newsom. As young as he looks, Newsom is one of the dead branches of tyranny. Governor Jared Polis of Colorado is a dead branch of the tyranny our forefathers fought against and overturned. These governors are not part of the future; they're part of the past.

Think about the Boston Tea Party and what triggered it. What these people are doing to our freedoms is just another dead branch to be cut away from our national tree. They've stolen our nation from us under the guise of protecting us. That's exactly what Hitler did. It's what Pol Pot did. It's what Mussolini did. It's what every tinpot dictator does. These liberal governors may not look like Mussolini or Pol Pot, but their policies are identical. "In the name of your safety, we will protect you," they say. "You may not go to church; you may not go to a restaurant; you may not get your nails done. We know what's best for you. Just be quiet and obey."

Now, if this was all validated by science, I might not be writing this. But it isn't. Every top scientist I was able to get on my radio show, *The Savage Nation,* all a hundred or a thousand times brighter than Dr. Slouchy, confirmed my view that selective quarantine was the proper response to this crisis. The only supposed scientists who believed locking down all of society and quarantining healthy people for the first time in history was the right thing to do were government scientists like Slouchy and the Scarf.

I used the word "scientist" rather loosely. Slouchy is a fake scientist who is nothing but a front for the pharmaceutical industry and has been since the AIDS epidemic. So many of these nobody health officials who could never make it in the private sector have been sitting in these bureaucracies for decades. These people are failures, losers, and nobodies, but not scientists. They're nothing but functionaries, Politburo members, like those in the ex–Soviet Union. These are the kinds of people who now control whether you can drive on the highway, go to a waffle restaurant, open your business, or send your child to school.

This is not my America. It's not any America I recognize.

It's time to cut the dead branches off the tree of liberty. It's time to tell them we, the American people, will not be oppressed by them. It's time to tell these sniveling bureaucrats, "You can take these outrageous laws and stick them where the sun doesn't shine. We've had enough!"

It's time.

THE DEMOCRATS KEEP STEALING
WITH BOTH HANDS

In the midst of all this tyranny you have the gangsters, the Democrats, trying to steal as much as they can while everyone is still shell-shocked by what has happened. After getting every bit of graft they could into the first $2.5 trillion bailout bill, they quickly put together a bill to hand out $3 trillion more.[16] They never miss an opportunity to rob the taxpayer. Of course, this bill was loaded up with the usual Democrat giveaways, including more spending on food stamps, student loan forgiveness, and yet more unemployment benefits at a time when some people are already reluctant to go back to work because their unemployment benefits are more money than their wages or salaries.[17]

Pelosi even snuck in stimulus money for illegal immigrants.[18] I kid you not. Republicans in the House tried to get that out of the bill but failed. What else is new? They're finally saying the right things about immigration but delivering on what they say about as well as they delivered "small government" when they had the House, Senate, and White House all at the same time.

It's hard to believe he Democrats have the audacity to do this. I keep asking myself, "When will this stop?" But I already know the answer. It will not stop unless we stop them.

All through this nightmare I kept asking myself why Pelosi and company would want to wreck the economy. What is in it for them? Why do they want us imprisoned? Why don't they want your little store or restaurant to reopen? Well, I looked into it. I did some research. During World War II, there were ration books. You needed ration cards to buy gasoline, tires, foods like sugar and coffee.[19] This was obviously a hardship, a sacrifice Americans made for the war effort. But Pelosi probably looks back nostalgically at this. This is the way she'd like us to live all the time, with the government telling us what goods we may consume and how many or how much.

That's basically how communist countries work. The government decides what goods will be produced and how much. Since there is no market price system, they have no idea whether they're producing the right products or the right quantities. Plus, communism has an incentive problem. Since nobody makes any more money by being more productive, nobody tries very hard. That all adds up to chronic shortages of everything, so the government must ration what the market provides free countries in abundance.

While done out of necessity, it works out well for totalitarians. A poor, starving population completely dependent upon the government for what they need to survive is very easy to control. And the constant shortages result in lots of opportunities for people to make fortunes on the black market. Pelosi isn't just the head thief of the Party of Larceny, she's also the picker of winners for a horde of crony capitalists. I'm sure there are many friends of the Democrat Party who would love either some government-created arrangement to be a monopolist provider of rationed goods or to be a player on the black market making a fortune while Pelosi looks the other way. There may even be opportunities to do both at the same time.

Now, the big lie was that we had to be locked down because they were afraid there would be too many cases at the same time, overwhelming the hospitals. You may not even remember that as the story has changed so many times over the course of this catastrophe. But, originally, the reason for the lockdowns was to prevent the hospitals from being swamped and running out of beds, ventilators, etc. Maybe that was a rational fear very early on. But long after we learned the mortality rate of this virus was more like .1–.4 percent, as opposed to the 3.4 percent reported early in the crisis, the policy remained the same. The lockdowns continued long after it was apparent that the concern that supposedly necessitated them was unwarranted.

That's not to mention that there was never any scientific rationale for these lockdowns to begin with. By early May, after people had been locked down in New York State for well over a month, it came out that 66 percent of all new coronavirus cases were people who had stayed home just as Governor Cuomo ordered. Another 18 percent were people in nursing homes, who were not only confined to the building but prohibited to have any visitors.[20] That means 84 percent of the new cases were people who had sheltered in place, just as Cuomo wished, yet they still contracted the virus. Only two percent of new cases were people who had congregated against the governor's orders and Dr. Slouchy's advice.

WHAT WILL AMERICA LOOK LIKE A YEAR FROM NOW?
So, we knew by May 6 that the lockdowns weren't working, but these fanatical, fascist governors kept extending them anyway. These dictators, either consciously or not, want to see the population reduced to dependence. They want to transform America from a nation of small towns, small

businesses, and a prosperous, independent middle class to a Third World socialist hellhole with only two classes: the poor and the party.

That's what life was like in the Soviet Union. Do you think there weren't rich people there? Do you think Joseph Stalin lived in a poor, low-cost apartment like the slaves he ruled over? Of course not. He lived in luxury, making use of dozens of "dachas" or summer homes when not in his luxury apartment in the Kremlin. If you were a high-ranking party member in the Soviet Union, you lived like royalty. If you were not, you scratched out a subsistence living and kept your head down lest you ran afoul of the party and heard a knock on your door during the night.

How can anyone not see that this is where we're headed? The middle class is being destroyed. The multinational corporations, overwhelmingly run by "woke" liberals, are being bailed out while independently owned small businesses are targeted for destruction. You don't need an MBA from Wharton to know how this turns out. The multinationals will acquire all the market share being lost by your local restaurants, barbershops, music stores, shoe stores, auto repair shops, and theaters. There will be nothing left owned by the people who live in your neighborhood. It will all be owned by Wall Street and foreign elites who are free to buy as much stock in those companies as they wish.

The Steve Walkers of the world will become slaves to these faceless giants, not because being an employee means being a "wage slave," as the left often puts it, but because the customers their employers are serving were stolen from them. They didn't lose their businesses to honest competition but to government interference on a scale hardly seen in the worst dictatorships in history.

This is what awaits us, America, if we do not resist. We will be reduced to an impoverished, joyless existence wearing face masks, suspicious of our neighbors, working for distant elites who own everything and live by a much different set of rules. Like the ranking party members in the old Soviet Union, they will not suffer with the rest of us. "Social distancing" isn't a problem when you can afford to pay for accommodations in restaurants and other public entertainment venues that can survive at half capacity or less, so no one is within six feet of anyone else. No, the beautiful people aren't going to suffer. You are.

The only caveat I will provide to this grim look into the future is Officer Greg Anderson's warning. There are still patriots in this country who will not go gently into that good night. Right now, the shows of arms are largely symbolic, but don't kid yourself that it will end there. Remember, the American colonists were reluctant to go to war with their own British government until the government put them in a position where they felt they had nothing to lose.

I pray to God our government doesn't put our bold peasantry in that position.

FOUR

HIJACKING MARTIN LUTHER KING'S DREAM

As the ship that was our civilization sank, we sat in the stern listening as the band played on. They were playing selections from the opera *Pagliacci* ("Clowns") by Ruggero Leoncavallo. Thus, did we play our own roles in that divine comedy called America.

It's hard to believe that when 2020 started, we were in the middle of the greatest economy the country had ever seen. By the time it was half over, we had a wrecked economy, burning cities, looted stores, and those not participating in the mayhem stalking our sidewalks in masks.

How could all of this happen in such a short time? You really must go back to before the coronavirus. It started with the phony impeachment created by Nancy Pelosi, based on bogus charges. We lived through that while all of Australia was on fire, the first set by arsonists.[1] California suffered a wildfire outbreak this year as well, also possibly caused by arson. Arson has been the third-leading cause of wildfires in California over the past forty years, but no one in the liberal media pays attention to that.[2] Every wildfire must be the result of global warming. Or, maybe now it's Covid-19 that's starting the fires.

Then a Chinese virus started spreading in that country while the government lied to cover it up with help from the once-respected World Health Organization (WHO).[3] The pandemic then engulfed the world, causing entire nations to shut down with people locked up in their homes for months on end. These lockdowns caused massive unemployment and thousands of businesses to close for good. The stock market lost everything it had gained during Trump's presidency in just a few weeks.

Of course, we know Wall Street is never allowed to take losses. The rest of us lose all the time, but the white-shoe welfare queens will always be bailed out. So, the government created trillions more in debt while throwing money at the government-created depression, boosting up the stock market.

Just when we thought maybe the coronavirus would be the last straw, Americans watched a cop murder a man on video, starting a series of protests and riots all over America. The left was immediately activated. They certainly weren't going to miss an opportunity to accelerate their ongoing destruction of America. The street thugs were set loose to destroy businesses already on their last legs from being forcibly shut down for months. Democrat leaders at the state and municipal level tell police officers to stand down, to permit the looting and violence to continue.[4] Meanwhile, another war on police erupts, with policemen shot and killed, or in one case, deliberately run down by a motor vehicle, all over the country.[5]

I was surprised to hear Trump give a press conference when the riots had just begun and talk about China and the World Health Organization (WHO) and not mention the riots going on in several U.S. cities.[6] I knew what was going on; I had told you what was going on. At a certain point, all administrations take on the same form. When they're in trouble, they need an external enemy in order to move forward. In this case, it was China.

Now, everything the president said about China that day was true. Everything he said about the WHO was true. It just wasn't the right time to be talking publicly about it. I've told you that people in the administration realize he may be in some trouble, given the bias in the media, the drift of the political world, and the fact that all incumbents get blamed for a national crisis. The Covid crisis is not the president's fault, but he will be blamed for it nonetheless.

So, the best thing is war with China. Even a nice, small war would draw the people together. That's what I'm afraid could happen, sooner or later. Meanwhile, American cities were burning again, something I had hoped we left behind with the last president.

You must understand what happened in Newark, New Jersey, years ago, in 1967. Newark was once a beautiful, middle-class city. Then, on July 12, 1967, a black cabdriver was beaten and arrested by two white police officers for a very minor traffic infraction. It happened in Newark's Central Ward area. This was before social media, but the word spread. According to History.com,

A crowd gathered outside police headquarters where the injured driver who was rumored to be dead was being held. Despite calls to remain calm, frustrated protestors, fed up with the lack of response to their concerns, began throwing rocks, breaking police station windows. Two days of looting followed—and when the looting stopped, the killing began, as New Jersey Governor Richard J. Hughes called in state troopers and the National Guard to restore order.[7]

By the time the carnage was over, there was massive property damage, hundreds of injuries, and loss of life. This previously beautiful city of Newark was broken forever. I hope that isn't the case for Minneapolis or Atlanta, but with the large numbers of white communists from universities in the area who are egging on the minorities, I don't know where this is going to end. I know Newark never recovered. We know what happened after the Rodney King affair.

Why did this happen when it did? On May 28, I tweeted the following:

COP KILLED BLACK MAN IN SLO MO-you hear the poor man crying for his mother! HE SHOULD BE TRIED FOR MURDER IN THE 1st DEGREE WITH ADDED CHARGES OF A HATE CRIME[8]

When I heard the man cry for his mother, part of me started to weep. He was dying, begging this bastard cop to stop killing him. Begging the cop to stop choking him to death with his knee. He was on the ground handcuffed, helpless. He couldn't fight back. And this homicidal maniac with a gun and a club put his knee on the man's neck, on his jugular vein. You could hear the man gasping, begging him to stop.

I told you what seeing a cow killed in a slaughterhouse did to me. If that got to me the way it did, you can imagine how I felt when I saw this man being choked to death for all the world to see. This big, strong man crying for his mother as his life was crushed out of him by a cowardly, homicidal maniac. This cop should have been charged with a hate crime because this was clearly race related. There was no question in my mind that was what I saw.

I really wondered that day whether President Trump should close down Twitter and arrest the heads of CNN and social media companies who were fanning the flames the same way Abraham Lincoln cut telegraph lines and arrested newspaper editors during the Civil War. Lincoln also arrested 13,000 civilians under martial law.

I realize that was wartime and the South at that moment was not considered part of the United States. But are you telling me we don't have a civil war going on in this country now? Is the left not as much a foreign nation as the Confederates were in 1862? In 2014, I published the first in a sequence of very important books, with titles that are also very important and will not be forgotten. The title of that first book in the sequence was *Stop the Coming Civil War*. I had planned to call the book simply, "The Coming Civil War," but my editors pleaded with me to modify it. So I added "Stop."

The truth is we've been in a civil war since 1967, when the hippies invaded the media and the colleges, beginning the long march toward outright communism. Don't kid yourself that they're not behind these riots. They are. Still, I said the cop in the George Floyd case should be charged with first-degree murder and a hate crime.

No one in the media has supported the police more than I have. I know they're the only thing standing between us and total chaos and mayhem. It's not an exaggeration to say that without law and order, that is, the safeguarding of life and property against exactly what went on in Minneapolis and several other cities earlier this year, there is no civilization.

Yes, civilization depends upon protecting life *and* property. More than two thousand years ago, Cicero went so far as to say safeguarding private property was the whole reason governments are formed.

> For the chief purpose in the establishment of constitutional state and municipal governments was that individual property rights might be secured. For, although it was by Nature's guidance that men were drawn together into communities, it was in the hope of safeguarding their possessions that they sought the protection of cities.[9]

Once private property is no longer safe, civilization is gone. I want you to remember that every time a left-wing television anchor or reporter euphemizes the wanton destruction of property as simply people expressing their anger at institutional injustice. Destroying the property of innocent third parties is not a legitimate form of protest. It is a crime that should be punished severely. I was angry myself when I saw the George Floyd video, and I'm still saying the anarchists who took advantage of the general anger over it to burn down Minneapolis, Atlanta, and several other cities should be thrown in jail for as long as the law will allow.

Of course, every big story since Donald Trump won the 2016 election has been surrounded by a blizzard of fake news, but I have to hand it to the crazed liberal media for the whopper they laid on us during the Minneapolis riots. This media had the temerity to suggest that these particular riots, no different from a dozen others over the past several years that were all funded, organized, and executed by left-wing agitators, were the work of "white supremacists."

According to this conspiratorial fever dream, white supremacists were inciting the minority communities to riot to somehow advance their agenda. This started when Minnesota governor Tim Walz said during a press conference that he had heard "unconfirmed reports that gangs of white supremacists are taking advantage of the anarchy unfolding in Minneapolis to create more chaos."[10] The story then got real legs when St. Paul mayor Melvin Carter announced that all the arrests made the first day of the riots were of people from out of state.[11]

Well, once those two statements hit that sewer of the mind called "Twitter," one of the more idiotic conspiracy theories in human history was born. It didn't matter that Carter retracted his statement the next day after a local news outlet looked at the county jail's roster and reported that nearly everyone arrested in fact lived in Minnesota.[12] Liberals still maintained that not only were there white supremacists participating in the riots; they were *behind* the riots. This was a plot to make minorities look bad so the white supremacists could . . . what?

Don't expect a liberal conspiracy theory to make sense. That's not a necessary part of their ideology. In fact, it's better if the theory doesn't make sense because liberalism itself doesn't make sense. It's a mental disorder, not a consistent philosophy. That "white supremacy" even makes the news tells you these people have no connection to reality.

I'm not saying there were no white supremacists rioting in Minneapolis. Neither am I denying there is a white supremacist movement in the United States. But it's a movement made up of an exceedingly small number of losers who are going nowhere politically. The vast majority of people the left calls "white supremacists" are no such thing. Most true white supremacists are people nobody ever heard of.

I shouldn't have to write this, but white supremacy has a definition. It describes a political system where there is a different set of rules for people based on their race. In a white supremacist society, there are laws on the books that grant privileges to white people that are denied to others. There are laws on the books that prohibit members of other races from doing things white people are allowed to do. That is a white supremacist society. South Africa under apartheid was a white supremacist society. The old Jim Crow South was white supremacist in effect, even though they tried to hide that with the "separate but equal" nonsense.

America today is not a white supremacist country.

As I said, this wasn't the first time there had been riots in the streets of American cities. They became part of the normal course of business when the Marxist Obama was in office, all but declaring open season on the police and carte blanche for Black Lives Matter and other George Soros–funded communist terrorist organizations to throw our cities into chaos. So, I generally support the police even if I don't support the police officer who murdered George Floyd.

This brings me to the next book in the sequence I've been talking about, which was called *Stop Mass Hysteria*. It was dedicated to the men and women of law enforcement who, as I wrote "are on the front lines protecting the rest of us from the violent, radical, left-wing street criminals whose goal is to tear our society to pieces." Obviously, suggesting my position on George Floyd's killer was motivated by any kind of an anti-cop bias is ludicrous.

But even among the best, you have the worst. And that day, we saw the worst. It reminded me of what I had written in *Stop Mass Hysteria* a few years before:

> Hatred is in the air. We are living in an age of hate, in which mental pollution is worse than air pollution. The most accessible and comprehensive of all unifying agents, hatred is spreading like a virus into all-too-willing hosts.[13]

I wrote those words two years ago. Unfortunately, they were prescient. I have been watching the results of the hatred that's been building in this country for a long time. I also shared a quote from Thomas Jefferson in that book that couldn't fit what we're going through better.

As Jefferson wrote, "I really look with commiseration over the great body of my fellow citizens who, reading newspapers, live and die in the belief that they have known something of what has been passing in the world in their time."[14]

Couple those timeless words with the idiots on Twitter and Facebook whose entire knowledge of the world around them can be expressed in the 280 words Twitter allows in a single tweet. It just goes to show that Jefferson's words are as true today as when he wrote them in 1807.[15]

When President Trump suggested that if left-wing governors and mayors couldn't put a stop to the violence and destruction—assuming they were really even trying—he would send in federal troops to quell the riots; his own secretary of defense, Mark Esper, publicly broke with the president, saying the use of troops was unnecessary.[16] Esper's predecessor, former general James Mattis, took that opportunity to break his own silence and call the president a "threat to the Constitution."[17]

Believe it or not, all that happened by June 3. It wasn't even summer yet and we were already a nation in chaos, with hurricanes in Florida, tornadoes in the Midwest, and earthquakes in California all still on the horizon. Now we're heading into flu season again, facing the second wave of Covid-19 and the likely overreaction by left-wing dictators great and small all over the country. Short of a foreign army successfully invading this continent, America could not look more like a broken nation.

It's easy to put all the blame for letting the street thugs get out of control on left-wing mayors and governors. But did the federal government do enough? Should Trump have sent in federal troops, regardless of what his establishment defense secretary had to say? My first instinct was that he should, although I had a change of heart on this and not because my heart bled for the looters. Sending in troops was just what the masterminds of these riots would want. That would allow them to paint Trump as a fascist dictator and any harm done to looters who weren't white as racism.

You must understand something: thugs do not respond to talk. I know you don't want to hear that. I know you don't want to live in an America where you have to see that. Neither do I. But neither do I want to see the carnage and cities burning we've seen during these riots.

How do you feel when you see these skinny, white punks from the suburbs, dressed in black over their mother's underwear, breaking into stores and stealing at will, while the police who could otherwise stop them are emasculated by the vermin who run these left-wing cities? How do you feel about seeing looters roll up in Rolls-Royces to ransack upscale shops? You have to ask yourself whether you would rather see all that than see these thugs get what they deserve.

Booker T. Washington, the great African American educator, author, and advisor to presidents, once wrote,

> There is another class of colored people who make a business of keeping the troubles, the wrongs, and the hardships of the Negro race before the public. . . . Some of these people do not want the Negro to lose his grievances, because they do not want to lose their jobs.[18]

Here was a man who was born a slave on a tobacco plantation in the Virginia hills. He didn't run around screaming for reparations, or blaming "whitey" for anything, even though he had legitimate grievances with those who had enslaved him.

THE DREAM IS OVER

Let me share a more recent quote from another great African American:

"I have a dream that one day in Alabama, with its vicious racists, with its governor having his lips dripping with the words of interposition and nullification, one day right there in Alabama little black boys and black girls will be able to join hands with little white boys and white girls as sisters and brothers."—Martin Luther King Jr. (1963)[19]

I was a young man when Martin Luther King Jr. gave his "I Have a Dream" speech on the steps of the Lincoln Memorial. It stands today as one of the greatest political speeches in American history. I was stirred then, as a young teacher, and am still stirred when I hear it played back today. What happened to his words, his ideals? What happened to his dream of brotherhood and sisterhood under God? Today, the civil rights movement he led has been hijacked by revolutionary communists.

Do you think Dr. King would approve of what has gone on in our cities this year—the looting, the burning, and the suggestion that police departments should be defunded? After the trillions of dollars that have been spent, the illegal, immoral affirmative action programs that have been put in place in hiring and scholarships, we still have riots and looting. We still have systemic hatred toward white people. Was King's speech a vision of future reality or was it always wishful thinking?

There are many left-wing organizations, hate groups, and powerful individuals fomenting hatred right now, including, unfortunately, Oprah Winfrey. Winfrey is a billionaire who had the nerve to put out a show on systemic racism.[20] It's hard not to gasp when you hear someone in her position make believe she's part of a radical movement. The day after her hate rally, I tweeted this:

BILLIONAIRE OPRAH SCREAMS ABOUT 'SYSTEMIC RACISM' -- GUESS SHE WOULD BE A TRILLIONAIRE IN A FAIR SOCIETY[21]

Yes, that was sarcasm. But seriously, how much more could she want? She's a talented woman who got where she did through talent, drive, and brains. Where else could she have become a billionaire? In what other country could she have done better than she has here?

Winfrey isn't alone. You're not hearing Martin Luther King's words in the print media, either, these days. As painful as it is sometimes, I read them all. And they're all fomenting revolution through their rhetoric. For me, it's nothing new. I've seen this from the left all my life. We again have the insane suggestion of paying reparations for slavery. A bill to study how this could be done passed the California Assembly in June, while fires from the recent spate of riots were still smoldering.[22] Of course senile Joe Biden was quick to jump on the bandwagon, saying he'd support paying reparations if "there are ways to get direct payments for reparations."[23]

Sure, there's a way, Joe. You rob innocent taxpayers and cut checks to your voting blocs. You don't need a study to figure that out. Just do us all a favor and tell me who should be responsible to pay for this, since no living American has ever owned a slave.

Yes, many early Americans owned slaves. No one denies that. But slavery was not invented in America. It was the status quo all over the world, including in the countries from which the first slaves came. Bondage slavery existed in almost every society going back to ancient times. I studied quite a few cultures during my time in academia and have read a lot of history outside of my formal studies, and I don't know of a tribe or a culture that did not at one time engage in slavery.

I know many liberals believe the Scandinavian countries were established in the 1970s, when they decided to adopt socialism, and born out of whole cloth as a paradise where everyone is peaceful and loving. I'd like to remind them Scandinavia was once ruled by pirates we call the "Vikings." In addition to the pillaging and murdering they are so famous for, they also enslaved people. They bought and sold people just as every other culture did at one time. That's how Denmark, Norway, Finland, and Sweden were really established. They are the descendants of slave-owning Vikings.

Today, the Vikings are long gone. The country has been taken over by radical feminist leftists. I'm not sure how that happened. How does a nation devolve from one extreme to another like that? Where have the men gone? There must be a few Vikings left in Scandinavia but where are they? It's not that I'd like to see the killing and the pillaging come back, but certainly a little "manly firmness," as Jefferson put it, would do all the Scandinavian countries a world of good. But I suppose that's why Scandinavians don't have to apologize for their slaveholding ancestors. If you flood your country with immigrants, erase your borders, language, and culture, and pay out enough welfare, you're off the hook for slavery.

Here in America, we're not quite there yet. Not only are there some patriots left in the population, but we had the nerve to elect Donald Trump president. I'm not sure that isn't worse than slavery to the left. And since the day he won that election, we've endured a nonstop assault on civilization itself, based on fomented hatred over phony victimization. First, it was the women with the vagina hats. Remember them? Trump had barely got his hand off the Bible at his inauguration when hundreds of thousands of women cheered on Madonna as she said she thought about blowing up the White House.[24]

Today, we have Black Lives Matter organizing "protests" where buildings really do get blown up, or at least burned down. This is due, they say, to "systemic police racism."

I saw through Obama the day he arrived on the scene. Here was a man who said he never paid much attention to his race until he went to Columbia University. He said he got a lot of notice when he began espousing the black power movements' rhetoric. Then, he said, the kids really paid attention to him and looked up to him. So, he got more into it.

America is the least racist nation on the planet. I want to remind you that Barack Obama, our first "African American president," got elected because white people voted for him. In case you forgot, white people are still the majority in America. That means you don't get elected in America unless white people vote for you. Enough voted for Barack Obama to send him to the White House.

What a salesman he was. Even I believed him when he gave those speeches at the beginning. He sounded so sincere about all the good he was going to do for America. And like all liberals, he came to Washington to do good and he did very well indeed. He came in middle class and left worth tens of millions.[25]

So, you have an African American president in office at the time of the ambush murder of five Dallas police officers in July 2016. During the memorial service for these officers, Obama said that African American children were right to fear they will be killed by police officers whenever they go outside.[26] This is the day of the funeral for those five Dallas cops. You tell me: Did that help advance Martin Luther King's dream of universal brotherhood or stoke mutual fear and suspicion between people of different races?

Fast-forward to this year. Minnesota governor Tim Walz, one of the greatest embarrassments in the history of that state, denounced the "stain" of "fundamental institutional racism" on law enforcement.[27] "Institutional racism" and "systemic racism" are popular terms thrown around by the radicals, repeated ad nauseam to explain outcomes they don't like. But does it exist? Not according to Heather Mac Donald of the *Wall Street Journal*, who writes that a "solid body of evidence finds no structural bias in the criminal justice system with regard to arrests, prosecution, or sentencing."[28] She has the data, which says crime and suspect behavior, rather than race, determine most police behavior.

In 2019, police shot 1,004 people, most of whom were armed or otherwise a threat to the safety of the officers. About 23 percent of those were African American. Now, the race-baiters would say that is evidence itself, since African Americans only make up about 12–13 percent of the population. But that's not a valid conclusion. There are all sorts of factors that have to be controlled to look at this scientifically.

Mac Donald says that the 23 percent number is actually *less* than the African American crime rate would predict.

In 2018, the last year for which there are statistics, African Americans were 53 percent of known homicide offenders in the United States and committed about 60 percent of the robberies. I know those numbers may be embarrassing to many liberals, but facts are facts. They don't lie. Here's another fact: a police officer is 18½ times more likely to be killed by a black male than an unarmed black male is to be killed by a police officer.[29]

I don't recall Oprah covering any of these statistics on her show. She should do another show that tells the truth as a form of apology to the millions of people who believe everything she said in the first one. If she won't take my advice, maybe she should ask billionaire white man David Geffen, on whose yacht she vacationed with other billionaires last year.[30] She should ask him if he thinks it's a good idea for her to continue to scream "systemic racism" and what he thinks will happen if she keeps fanning the flames and throwing lighter fluid on the charcoal.

DEFUND THE POLICE?

As I watched American cities burn, stores looted, and citizens assaulted, one burning question seemed to beg itself. What do these people want? They say they're angry about "systemic racism," but what concrete action could their city, state, or federal governments take that would appease them?

Now, the real answer to that question is "nothing." Nothing anyone can say or do will ever appease these malcontents because deep down, racism isn't the real problem to them. It's our civilization itself. It's private property and free enterprise they ultimately want to destroy and until they succeed, even a black president, a black governor, a black mayor, and African Americans running the local school board won't satisfy them. We know this, of course, because we've had all of the above and here they are still destroying our cities.

They did come up with something, though, and that was to "defund the police." It took several days before even the people spouting this nonsense knew what they meant by it, but it finally metamorphized into taking money away from police departments and spending it on social workers, community programs, and public schools.

Kamala Harris wants to be vice president. Now, she's a former prosecutor, a relatively tough one, by the way. She's an intelligent woman and should be espousing unity, the message of Martin Luther King Jr. Instead, she sounds like a child. I don't know who is advising her, but at one point she came out with this little gem.

> "The status quo has been to determine and create policy around the idea that more police equals more safety. And that's just wrong. You know what creates greater safety? Funding our public schools, so that, currently, two-thirds of our public-school teachers don't have to come out of their own back pocket to pay for school supplies."[31]

Let me take a moment to address the shibboleth of funding public schools. I'm willing to bet most Americans don't know minority students receive more funding per student than nonminority students. That's not what we're led to believe, but it's true. The Brookings Institution conducted a study of precisely this and found the opposite result of what even they were expecting. Among their findings:

> In richer districts, poor and Hispanic students receive more school resources, relative to their non-poor and white peers in the same districts.
>
> Districts with more school segregation—whether socioeconomic or racial—tend to spend more on poor and minority students relative to nonpoor and white students.
>
> Black and Hispanic students receive relatively fewer resources in districts where black or Hispanic family income is more equal to (or even higher than) white family income.[32]

In other words, counter to the "systemic racism" allegation, rich white school districts and more segregated school districts spend more money on minority students than they do on white students. It is in those districts where Black and Hispanic family income is equal or greater, meaning minority families would have more political clout, that minority students receive less.

How can this be? CNN (the Communist News Network) tells me America is racist. Well, it turns out that not only is America not racist when it comes to public education, but it is far more benevolent to the poor than we're told as well. The richer people in a given school district tend to use their political clout to direct more resources toward the poorer students, whether the richer families in that district are white and the poor families nonwhite *or vice versa.*

I already knew this. I'm a former social worker and studied this twenty years ago. At the time, I was shocked to find basically the same results in my own Marin County as Brookings found overall. Unfortunately, throwing more money at minority or poorer students does not result in better grades. So, this myth about less funding for minority students is a lie, like everything else these radical leftists say.

As far as Harris's claim that more police doesn't result in more safety, 80 percent of Americans disagree with her. A poll taken before George Floyd's death by the National Sheriffs Association showed that eight in ten Americans wanted to either maintain or even increase police funding.[33] But that all changed after the horrific killing of Floyd by a Minneapolis cop, right?

Wrong. A Rasmussen Report survey in early June, at the height of the protests over Floyd's killing, found that just 17 percent of Americans think there are too many police. And here's the real kicker: only 27 percent of blacks surveyed think there are too many police![34] So, these radical communists who have hijacked the civil rights movement don't remotely represent even most black people in this country.

Ironically, it's always the rich who foment communist revolutions. Karl Marx came from a comfortable, upper-middle-class family. Even though he was a ne'er-do-well for most of his adult life, he sponged off his friend Friedrich Engels, who came from an even richer family. Vladimir Lenin also came from a comfortable middle-class family. His father was a self-made man who rose from serfdom to get a university education and eventually become a director of public schools and a nobleman. His mother came from a wealthy family. A lot of these revolutionaries were lawyers, too, just like Kamala Harris. Fidel Castro was a lawyer who came from a wealthy family. His father made a fortune in sugarcane.

It's an old story. The parents work seven days a week building a business or bettering themselves to provide a comfortable life for their children, but the children grow up spoiled and become malcontents. I worked my hind end off to provide my son a comfortable life and he repaid me by becoming even more successful than I am. So, I must have done something right raising him, although the success belongs to him.

CONGRESSIONAL COSTUME PARTIES

Meanwhile in Congress, Nancy Pelosi decided the best way for her legislators to help a country coming apart at the seams was to have a costume party. What a stunt that was. I couldn't believe how stupid was the pandering these phonies were willing to undertake. Before proposing new legislation for "police reforms," Pelosi, Schumer, and other Democrats donned scarves made of traditional African Kente cloth and kneeled for the eight minutes and forty-six seconds the insane cop in Minneapolis had his knee on George Floyd's neck.[35]

Well, actual black people found this pandering by rich, white liberals offensive. Author Obianuju Ekeocha told them to stop virtue signaling and treating Africans like cute children.[36] Nana Efua Mumford, executive assistant to the *Washington Post*'s Editorial Board, wrote, "My traditional cloth is not a prop."[37] It turns out even liberal black people don't like to be patronized.

There is a humorous angle to all this. Eighty-year-old Nancy Pelosi needed help to get back to her feet after kneeling that long.[38] Former fatso Jerry the Nebbish Nadler didn't kneel at all, citing "physical limitations."[39] What's the matter, Jerry? Did you do too much damage to your knees before having your stomach sown shut?

A hundred years from now, I hope people can look back and laugh at some of the nonsense these morons engaged in, just as we might at what was going on in Congress or the British Parliament one hundred years ago. The one problem is that if they pull off their revolution, and end up rounding people up and killing them, as all successful left-wing revolutions eventually do, even Nebbish Nadler won't be funny anymore.

That is not hyperbole. If you think "it can't happen here," just take a step back and look at what is already occurring before your very eyes. You have violent radicals literally burning down buildings in American cities. You have liberal governors and mayors telling police to stand down while at the same time signing stricter and stricter gun control measures. Small businesses are being destroyed; their market share effectively handed to multinational corporations that now openly endorse radical communist hate group Black Lives Matter. Big Tech is erasing your presence online, the primary conduit for conversation in twenty-first-century America. Disarmed, impoverished, and defenseless, it is but a small step for them to demand obedience to their every dictate or make you disappear completely—either literally or figuratively.

It *is* happening here.

FIVE

A PUBLIC HEALTH DISASTER

I was never in the buffoon camp. That is, I've never said Covid-19 was "just like the flu," exaggerated by the Democrats just to harm Donald Trump's reelection chances. This virus is not just like the flu. It kills more people and it kills some people the flu doesn't. It is a dangerous virus that must be taken seriously.

That said, we now understand that this epidemic is no different from others. No, that doesn't understate its danger. Other epidemics have been dangerous. But when you take a step back and look at this with a scientist's eyes, it is very much like past epidemics.

First, it is clustered in urban centers, as have been all epidemics in recorded history. I should know; I have studied epidemics since graduate school. Yet the demonic and power-mad petty bureaucrats in the NIH and CDC, and the governors in many states, have made everyone suffer equally, whether they live in an urban center or not. It made no sense to close down all of New York State when everyone knows the disease is clustered in New York City. It made no sense to close down rural Northern California when the disease was clustered in Los Angeles and San Francisco.

So why did they do it? The answer to that question is what I call "public health affirmative action," assuming they did this knowingly. They didn't want to be seen as "discriminatory" or "racist" to the largely minority communities in the urban centers. That's likely what would have happened if they had limited the closures to the cities and left the largely Caucasian rural areas open.

That doesn't make it right, of course. The risk that the identity politics monster that people like Andrew Cuomo and Gavin Newsom helped create might turn on them for a change, instead of the conservatives they created it to destroy, does not justify the devastation these maniacs have unleashed on civilization. If I were so cowardly as to let something like that stop me from doing the right thing, I would have been off the air twenty years ago.

The other possibility is no more encouraging. They could simply be so ignorant of the facts of this or any epidemic that they locked down entire states in a panic, imprisoning entire populations without any thought to the unintended consequences. Peer-reviewed studies have shown there are more suicides during recessions.[1] How many more will occur when this full-on depression is at its nadir? How many more drug overdoses, deaths from untreated diseases due to loss of employer health insurance, and other premature deaths will occur as a result of the "cure being worse than the disease"?

I can't give you a number, but I can tell you the number cryptofascist governors are estimating when they issue their one-size-fits-all edicts: zero. They're not even contemplating what unintended effects their policies might have. Governments never do.

You can afford to make colossal mistakes like that when you are not accountable for the results. It's not like governors or public health bureaucrats ever face any legal ramifications for the calamities they cause. In the private sector, a mistake like this that costs people their lives or their livelihoods has consequences. People get fired. People get sued. Often, people go to jail, even if there was no malicious intent. Consequences are often disproportionately severe in the private sector, thanks to antibusiness sentiment among the envious public.

But in the public sector, there are no consequences. As we've seen repeatedly throughout history, you can cause massive social and economic devastation and the worst that happens to you is you may lose the next election. Maybe. In one-party states like New York or California, you're for the most part insulated even from this.

Ironically, in an apparent moment of clarity, New York governor Cuomo admitted his universal lockdown of New York State's economy and population was wrong. Believe it or not, this is a direct quote:

> What we did was we closed everything down. That was our public health strategy, just close everything. All businesses, all workers, young people, old people, short people, tall people, every school, close everything.

If you re-thought that, or had time to analyze that public health strategy, I don't know that you would say, "quarantine everyone." I don't even know that was the best public health strategy. Young people then quarantined with older people was probably not the best public health strategy.[2]

Well, look who just caught up. The only problem is he didn't catch up, even after making this statement during a press conference on March 26. Two months later, all of New York State was still locked down. Now, whether his admission resulted from some genuine introspection or whether he was already starting to read the writing on the wall in terms of the economic devastation he was visiting on New Yorkers is something only the meatball man himself can tell you. But how do you make a statement like that and not modify your statewide shutdown order?

As I said, you can behave this way when there are no consequences.

I had been calling for selective quarantines at least as far back as mid-February. But what do I know? I've only been studying epidemics for over forty years after earning a PhD in an interdisciplinary field that includes epidemiology. Had the pointy-headed bureaucrats in our sad excuse for public health agencies listened to me from the beginning, this nation would not have lost its Constitution and its economy.

What do I mean by "selective quarantine"?

It's just what it sounds like. You don't lock everyone in their homes; you quarantine those whose quarantining will protect them or protect the public. You start with those already known to be infected and those who are exhibiting symptoms. You move on to those at high risk of serious illness or death if infected: the elderly, those with underlying medical conditions or compromised immune systems. And let me add those the media won't mention, whom good little liberals don't want you to talk about: the homeless and illegal immigrant populations.

The homeless population is like a petri dish for a new virus.

TRUMP DEFENDS OUR BORDERS

That's not to say the news was all bad, especially concerning the president's own performance after the outbreak. The first thing he did was the right thing: he defended our borders. That might sound strange to some people in the context of a public health problem, if they haven't listened to my show or read my previous books. I've been talking about the dangers to public health from illegal immigration for decades.

Borders aren't just there to protect us from invading armies, whether they wear uniforms or call themselves "undocumented immigrants." They're also there to protect us from diseases that are not native to our population. If you just graduated from college with $150,000 in debt and a degree in global warming, you probably haven't heard this, but protecting public health was once one of the chief objectives at Ellis Island. Immigrants seeking to enter this country used to literally be herded through cattle pens and were seen by two separate U.S. Public Health Service (PHS) medical officers. The second examiner looked for anything the first may have missed.[3]

That's not a story invented by conservative talk radio. That's according to a peer-reviewed article in the *American Medical Association Journal of Ethics*. The article goes on to say that although the stated mission of the PHS was narrowly defined as preventing diseases from entering through the border, the PHS officers who did the screenings took the initiative to look for more.

> In their eyes, the goal was to prevent the entrance of undesirable people—those "who would not make good citizens." In the context of industrial-era America, immigrants who would wear out prematurely, requiring care and maintenance rather than supplying manpower, would not make "good" citizens.[4]

Imagine public health officers screening immigrants not only for diseases but for other signs they would be a burden on society rather than a contributor. That was before borders were declared racist and enforcing immigration laws fascist. Now, we can all enjoy not only demographic diversity but disease diversity. Thanks to Obama's pen and phone immigration policies, we are now seeing previously eradicated or nearly eradicated diseases making a comeback in America. They include tuberculosis, measles, and the polio-like disease, EV-D68, which I talked about in my book, *Diseases Without Borders*. We've even seen cases of the plague in some parts of America.

Luckily, elections matter. President Trump acted swiftly to declare a public health emergency and ban virtually all travel from China for non-U.S. citizens or permanent residents. Even U.S. citizens faced a mandatory fourteen-day quarantine if they were reentering the United States after visiting China's Hubei Province.[5] U.S. citizens who traveled anywhere in China were subject to a screening upon arrival back in the States and fourteen days of heightened monitoring.

Now, in any sane country, this would be a noncontroversial response to a dangerous pandemic. But not among the "woke" here in the USSA. "Coronavirus Outbreak Risks Reviving Stigma for China," bellowed the *New York Times*.[6] That bastion of objective reporting CNN said the policy could backfire for the same reasons.[7] "Such restrictions can have the effect of increasing fear and stigma, with little public health benefit," said World Health Organization director general Tedros Adhanom Ghebreyesus, according to CNN.[8]

Obviously, the Democrat Party included "stigma" in their talking points against Trump's response to the coronavirus.

THE CDC DROPS THE BALL

I've been complaining the CDC is fundamentally broken for most of my media career. Unfortunately, it takes more than electing one man to fix it. Trump closed the borders to travel from China and handed the ball to his secretary of health and human services, Alex Azar. Azar directed the CDC to begin tests in five cities and prepared a statement to the U.S. Senate on what the administration's next steps would be. So far, so good.

That's when Azar found himself mired knee-deep in Swamp sludge. According to the *Washington Post*, the CDC pushed back on the wording of Azar's statement, asking him to "soften it."[9] Why? Because the CDC wasn't ready to execute what should have been a routine first step in dealing with a potential outbreak within our borders. It seems the tests they were supposed to administer in those five cities were producing inconclusive results due to "an unspecified problem with a compound." What does that mean? Who knows? It's cover-your-behind language for incompetence.

There was also infighting between agencies, particularly between the CDC and the Office of the Assistant Secretary for Preparedness and Response.[10] That should sound familiar. Remember 9/11? The Department of Homeland Security was formed ostensibly to deal with that problem among intelligence agencies. Well, here we see it all over again between public health and emergency response agencies.

To some extent, government will be government. You can't expect the kind of efficiencies you see in private business, where people stand to lose their own money. But is it too much to ask that a department called the "Centers for Disease Control and Prevention" at least be ready to *try* to control the spread and prevent new cases of a deadly disease, instead of quarreling with their fellow bureaucrats?

Trump's initial response was correct. China didn't like it, of course. Neither did the World Health Organization, which advised against any travel restrictions.[11] Those are two reasons you know it was the right call. For the World Health Organization in particular to be advising against what any public health official should learn in Epidemiology 101 is particularly disturbing.

I don't say that from an uninformed perspective. I earned my PhD in nutritional ethnomedicine, an interdisciplinary degree that includes elements of medical anthropology, ethnobotany, nutrition, and epidemiology, from the University of California, Berkeley. My doctoral thesis was published as a book, which is rare. So when I say, "Epidemiology 101," I'm talking about a course I actually took!

Back in February, I told my listeners the story of John Snow, now considered the "father of epidemiology." Snow was famous for tracing the origin of a cholera outbreak in 1854 London to a water pump that was drawing water from a polluted section of the Thames River. This was at a time when people didn't yet know germs caused diseases and were blaming "bad air" for the outbreak. Using a dot map, statistics, and deductive reasoning, Snow showed how all the cases were clustered around this one particular water pump.

Snow convinced local authorities to remove the handle of the water pump, ending the spread of the disease. Snow's work provided that a disease outbreak could be traced back to its source, the foundation of epidemiology. Now, here is what you don't need an advanced degree to know: once you have identified the source of an outbreak, you don't transport infected people out of the area and create multiple start points for new outbreaks. But that's just what the CDC has done in outbreak after outbreak, aided by Obama's Office of Refugee Resettlement, which transplanted illegal immigrants with infectious diseases all over the country.[12]

We're not seeing the same reasoning in terms of potentially infected foreigners under Trump. Given the choice between letting in an infected foreign national or tiptoeing around risking a "stigma" against Asians, Trump is risking the stigma. And guess what. If you asked any sane Asian American or even legal Asian immigrant which they'd rather have, the stigma or the coronavirus, my money is on them taking the stigma. These are the people who outperform everyone else in academics. They're not stupid and they're not complainers. They just achieve. That's why they're not on the Democrat Party's list of victim groups.

HOW BAD IS COVID-19?

It's understandably difficult for honest people to determine what the truth is about anything in our toxic political climate today. That's true for anything, including this pandemic, which is just beginning to get serious as of this writing. By the time you read this book, it may have spread to millions more people. Then again, there is always the chance it mutates into a less deadly strain or the authorities get their act together and do what needs to be done to contain the disease. I wouldn't bet on the latter scenario.

In February and March, we didn't know as much about Covid-19 as we do now. We didn't know if it was far deadlier than we were being led to believe or far less deadly. On March 6, 2020, the *New York Times* told you "health officials tend to put it somewhere within range of an unusually severe seasonal flu. Even in a global pandemic, it's expected to kill fewer people than the flu virus."[13] But on the same day it ran another article with startling numbers: the seasonal flu has a mortality rate of 0.1 percent; this coronavirus has a mortality rate of at least 1.4 percent.[14]

That would have made Covid-19 at least seven times deadlier than the seasonal flu, which kills between 290,000 and 650,000 people a year globally. Do the math. Take either one of those numbers and multiply by seven. Early reports showed a case fatality rate of between 2 percent and 4 percent, which would have been comparable to the case fatality rate for the 1918 Spanish flu pandemic. That one killed upward of fifty million people. Now, even a case fatality rate of 0.7 percent, or 7 out of every 1,000 people infected dying, should alarm us. We may now know the virus is nowhere near as deadly as we were led to believe. But at the time, it was irresponsible to not take it seriously.

Now, it's true that fatalities due to the disease have mostly been older people. China's Center for Disease Control did a study of over 70,000 cases and found no fatalities among children aged 0–9 years old. Most of the people who died were over sixty years of age.[15] So, it's true to say the greatest risk of the virus making you seriously ill or dying is for older people. But the last time I checked, older people were still *people*.

However, the mortality rate for a disease is not the only consideration. No, the coronavirus is not as deadly as Ebola or SARS, and is far less deadly than we were initially led to believe. But it has a high morbidity rate. There is a difference between morbidity rates and mortality rates. Morbidity means the duration of the infection and how long it debilitates an infected individual. For example, a disease that doesn't kill many people, but which renders bedridden for an extended period a high percentage of infected people, would be a disease with a low mortality rate, but a high morbidity rate. The CDC itself puts out a weekly bulletin called "Morbidity and Mortality."[16] They report the respective morbidity and mortality rates for various diseases, broken down by state.

While the mortality rate for Covid-19 is relatively low compared to some deadlier diseases, the morbidity rate is high.

Also, the reinfection rate of this coronavirus is very high. People have reported recovering from the virus and then becoming ill a second time. This is a very intelligent virus.

You may think viruses aren't intelligent, but the facts prove otherwise. Virologists will tell you that viruses are very intelligent; it's just a different kind of intelligence. According to research going back to the late 1990s, many viruses "have evolved defenses to help them evade the immune system. Viruses that cause infection in humans hold a 'key' that allows them to unlock normal molecules (called viral receptors) on a human cell surface and slip inside. Once in, viruses commandeer the cell's nucleic acid and protein-making machinery, so that more copies of the virus can be made."[17] So, scoff all you want. I prefer to grant viruses a healthy respect.

Let me be clear. I tried to inform people about the virus to help both the people and the president. That is what higher education is for: to help people, to bring them knowledge and enlightenment. No one downplaying the threat of this virus to the American public is doing the public or the president any favors. Sometimes you can tell who your real friends are by who tells you what you don't want to hear.

I fist bump under normal circumstances. Now, for a guy my age to fist bump is really odd. But people smile when I do so, saying, "that makes sense during an epidemic." I don't shake hands. I haven't for years, even before there was a coronavirus epidemic. One of the most primitive ways of transferring pathogens is shaking someone's hand.

As an aside, shaking hands is really a brutish custom anyway. It was originally a way to show people you weren't carrying a weapon. That's why it's customary to extend one's right hand to shake. Most people are right-handed, so by showing your open right hand, you were showing the person you greeted you weren't about to stab or bludgeon them. The actual shaking part of the custom was to shake loose any hidden weapons. Like I said, it's brutish and can be eliminated.

The Chinese don't shake hands. They have it right. They bow to each other and shake their own hands. Sometimes you'll see representations of Chinese men putting one hand over the top of their fist while they bow. This also relates to weapons. It is symbolic of covering one's weapon, showing one's intentions are peaceful. Or, you may see the Chinese putting their open hands together, the way we do when we pray. But you never see them shaking hands the way we do.

There is a reason for that. They've had many epidemics in China over the thousands of years their civilization has been around. They know better than to be brutish and idiotic about a simple greeting. They manage to show respect for one another without taking the risk of spreading what could be a deadly disease to the person they greet.

I don't touch light switches in public places, either. I don't lift the gasoline dispenser in a gas station with my bare hand. That's not only because I'm afraid of the pathogens, but also because I don't want the gasoline penetrating my skin.

Even before the politically-motivated lockdowns, people were changing their lifestyles in response to this pandemic. I can tell you anecdotally, based on what friends in San Francisco told me, that reservations for all the upscale restaurants were way down as of this writing. Restaurants in Chinatown suffered from a lack of customers in their restaurants as far back as February.

Let me repeat what I've been telling my listeners since this outbreak became publicly known: the virus itself was not about Donald Trump. Everything that happens in the world is not a plot by the New World Order or the Democrats or the lizard people to take down the Trump presidency. Was Russiagate? Yes. Was the dead-on-arrival impeachment scam? Yes. Was this virus created to hurt Donald Trump? No.

Initially, there was some good advice being given by governors of the states, Republican and Democrat, to help mitigate the public health damage. They weren't telling you to stay home from bars and restaurants and avoid gatherings of more than a few people to hurt Donald Trump. They were doing it on the advice of highly educated medical and public health officials to save lives and even greater damage to our society. Later, Democrat governors obviously politicized the crisis. There is a big difference between advising people to stay home voluntarily if they can and forcibly closing down virtually every business, church, and social gathering in the state.

In the book, *On Grief and Grieving,* David Kessler and Elisabeth Kübler-Ross talk about the five stages of grief. They are denial, anger, bargaining, depression, and acceptance. Well, their framework applies to this virus as well. This is like a meteor just fell out of the sky and slammed into a portion of our planet. It won't just affect the area it hits. It's going to affect much of the world. But there are a lot of know-nothing conservatives and MAGA-heads out there who are in the denial stage. They talk as if Covid-19 was invented to hurt Donald Trump.

Some may have progressed to the angry stage, but I don't know what they are going to do after that. Who will they bargain with? I suggest they skip bargaining and depression and move right to acceptance as quickly as possible. Covid-19 is real, and the president has handled it as well as anyone in his place could have. He quickly banned travel from China. He banned travel from Europe when it was evident their open-borders policy wasn't the best way to keep a dangerous virus from spreading. And when the time was right, he declared a national emergency, allowing his administration to make emergency funds available and clear away the red tape that was hindering his administration's response.

BATS OR BIOWEAPONS?

The truth is we still don't know the origin of this coronavirus. There are rumors it may have originated in a Chinese lab. I don't know if they're true, but it is curious that one day after a speech by Chinese president Xi Jinping on the need to contain the coronavirus, the Chinese Ministry of Science and Technology released a new directive titled: "Instructions on strengthening biosecurity management in microbiology labs that handle advanced viruses like the novel coronavirus."[18]

Guess where the only microbiology lab that handles these types of advanced viruses is located. If you said Wuhan, you guessed right. The only level 4 microbiology lab that is equipped to handle deadly coronaviruses is located there. It's called the National Biosafety Laboratory and it is part of the Wuhan Institute of Virology.[19]

There is other evidence the virus is a combination of three different viruses, which is very suspicious. It's not a virus that was known to science prior to this outbreak. That makes me wonder if it is engineered. However, even if it was engineered in a Chinese lab, it may not have been a deliberate attack on Europe and the United States. Not that I consider China above sacrificing tens of thousands of its own citizens, but it was more likely something that escaped from the lab in error, spreading to the population around the lab.

At this point, what good does it do us to know? The virus is real. It's here. And it may be coming back for round two this autumn. I suggest you take the advice I've given you in this chapter. Listen to people who are educated in medicine, epidemiology, and related sciences and not those with a degree in talk radio who never graduated from high school. Yes, the panic is overdone, but the precautions public health officials and some politicians are giving you is good advice.

CONTAGIOUS AFTER RECOVERY

You can take the attitude that you are young and strong and don't care if you get the virus. You'll be better in a few weeks and won't need to be hospitalized. "All I'll get is mild flu symptoms, what do I care?" Well, that may be true for some people. But even those whose symptoms are relatively mild can infect other people, including people they do care about. In fact, they may still be able to infect someone after they've recovered from the virus themselves.

Little attention has been paid to the follow-up on recovered patients. They did a small study in China, the results of which were published in the *Journal of the American Medical Association* in February.[20] It was an obscure article, a research letter, but it was of paramount importance and as of this writing I hadn't seen any reference to it by any of the experts.

It studied four patients who were exposed to the novel

coronavirus through their work as medical professionals. Three of the patients exhibited fever, cough, or both at onset, while one patient was initially asymptomatic.

Upon exposure, all four patients were given the RT-PCR test, which is the test for this coronavirus, and CT scans. The RT-PCR tests were positive, and the CT scans showed "ground-glass opacification or mixed ground-glass opacification and consolidation." The severity of the disease for all four was mild to moderate. All four were given antiviral treatments and recovered in 12 to 32 days, at which point all four had two consecutive negative RT-PCR test results.

So, if you're one of the deniers, the fake newsers, the hoaxers, you're telling yourself that even if you get it, you'll get over it. Not so fast. Let me let you in on what else the study found.

The RT-PCR tests were repeated 5 to 13 days later and guess what? All were positive. Over the next four to five days they repeated the tests three times, and all still came out positive. They tried an RT-PCR test using a test kit from a different manufacturer and the results were again positive for all patients.[21]

Even though these patients were no longer showing symptoms and their CT scans were clear, they were still testing positive for the virus. These findings suggest that at least some proportion of patients who have fully recovered from Covid-19 and are asymptomatic may be virus carriers. That's something to remember if you aren't overly worried about getting Covid-19 because you're young and strong. You might still infect others.

It also shows that the governors in many states telling their citizens to self-isolate early on were making a lot of sense.

That's because even though you might be asymptomatic, you may be a silent carrier of this virus. That doesn't mean it's a time for panic, but it is a time for common sense. Despite their later politicization and mishandling of the crisis, the advice they were giving in the early stages was common sense.

THE SORCERER'S APPRENTICE

If cooler heads ever prevail in the White House, they'll push the grandstander Anthony Fauci back into a laboratory where he belongs. I don't think he's seen the inside of a laboratory in longer than I have. This man is the P. T. Barnum of the coronavirus. He's a showman. Everywhere you turn, there he is, Fauci the savior. Enough already.

Fauci told Newsmax in January that although the virus had to be taken seriously and people should follow CDC guidelines, "This is not a major threat to the people of the United States and this is not something that the citizens of the United States should be worried about right now."[22] He said that on January 21.

On that very same day, I said the following on Twitter:

QUARANTINE! STOP ALL TRAVELERS FROM CHINA FROM ENTERING THE U.S./ common-sense means to protect Americans! CDC IS USELESS. RUN BY POLITICAL HACKS NOT PUBLIC HEALTH SERVANTS[23]

One of us was right that day and one of us was wrong. But it wasn't just that day. Two days later, on January 23, I tweeted this:

QUARANTINE! STOP TRAVELERS FROM CHINA
NOW! China using Quarantine in their own infected
cities! WHY IS CDC SO WORTHLESS? WHO IS
IN CHARGE IN THE U.S.? PRESIDENT TRUMP,
WAKE UP! DON'T LET THE EVIL PELOSI VILLAINS
DISTRACT YOU FROM PROTECTING US FROM THIS
EPIDEMIC. TRAVEL BAN NOW![24]

I've been consistent with my recommendations on this pandemic since at least late January. While Dr. Grouchy Fauci was saying this virus was nothing Americans should worry about, I was loud and clear that this indeed was something to worry about, even though that wasn't fashionable in conservative media circles. My recommendation then was the same as it is now: selective quarantine.

Fauci has been around in the NIH for over forty years. How does a man remain part of the bureaucracy that long? Let me tell you. Because he's part of the Swamp. Donald Trump came to Washington to drain the Swamp but there it is, bubbling at his right hand on television every day during his coronavirus press conferences. Next to Swamp creature Fauci is Swamp Sister Dr. Deborah Birx, the scarf lady. She doesn't even have a medical license anymore. It expired in 2014 and has not been renewed as of this writing.[25]

I warned Donald Trump how bad the NIH and CDC were back in 2015, when he first announced as a presidential candidate. They had already been useless organizations for a long time by then. Now, make no mistake. In these organizations you have some first-rate people. It's a lot like the FBI. The agents on the street are usually the best but the people on top of them are usually the worst. The directors are usually just political hacks who undermine the police every day of the week, taking the side of the criminal.

It's the same inside these large bureaucracies like the CDC and NIH. Whatever quality work might be done in the trenches at these agencies, political hacks like Dr. Slouchy nullify them with their self-aggrandizement and incompetence, two qualities both innate in the bureaucrat species and encouraged by a complete lack of accountability for their failures.

That reminds me of a story from back in the early 1980s. There was a health commissioner back then in France. I believe he oversaw the production of vaccines. Well, a vaccine came out that killed thousands of Frenchmen on his watch. That public health minister was put in prison. The French not only take their civil liberties very seriously, they hold their bureaucrats' feet to the fire. They don't let them get away with murder.

Here we have Dr. Slouchy. First, he told people not to worry. Go out; go to a ballgame. Don't wear a mask.[26] Then, he told us wearing a mask is "what you should be doing."[27] So, when was he wrong, when he told us to wear a mask or when he told us not to wear one? Because he was wrong on one of those occasions and should pay for it as did that French bureaucrat. He shouldn't have just been fired; he should have been charged. That's really the only way to hold bureaucrats accountable, because as we've seen, it's impossible to fire them.

The mask wasn't the only issue this pharmacy delivery boy flip-flopped on. On May 12, he told Congress that reopening the country too soon would be dangerous. He said the country would face more "suffering and death" if states moved to reopen too fast.[28] On May 22—just ten days later—this buffoon told CNBC that it was time to reopen the economy![29] He said staying locked down for too long could cause "irreparable damage" and that "now is the time, depending upon where you are and what your situation is, to begin to seriously look at reopening the economy, reopening the country to try to get back to some degree of normal."[30]

Is the man insane or an imbecile? Maybe he's starting down the road to senility. If so, he should stay on at the NIH even if Biden wins the election. We might as well have consistency between the White House and NIH.

While all of the above may be true, there is an explanation for Slouchy's flip-flopping that is even more frightening than stupidity, senility, or schizophrenia.

And don't think maneuvering isn't what Slouchy is doing every minute of every day. In addition to recognizing his incompetence, I've smelled a rat when it comes to this guy since the beginning. I pray Donald Trump doesn't trust this guy because he shouldn't. He should have been fired a long time ago.

That he's the darling of the media should be your first clue this man is no friend of the president. He told fake news virtuoso Jake Tapper, of all people, that more lives could have been saved if the president acted more quickly.[31] Sure, he hemmed and hawed a little and tried to make it look like he was answering reluctantly. But believe me, he knew what he was doing.

Maybe the president is on to him. I don't know. It certainly was no accident that the president retweeted a tweet defending him on this point that contained the hashtag "#FireFauci."[32]

Nevertheless, as late as June 18 this charlatan was still causing public confusion by casting doubt on whether the NFL could plan on having a season this year. The president weighed in with what should be an uncontroversial statement: "Tony Fauci has nothing to do with NFL Football."[33]

Dr. Slouchy should no longer have anything to do with the Trump administration, either, but apparently not even when a successful businessman runs the government can lifelong bureaucrats be fired for failure or insubordination. Both Dr. Slouchy and the Scarf had time during their pressing duties to tell NBC that the president should not hold his first campaign rally.[34] Isn't that convenient?

We no longer have public health institutions in this country. We have political health institutions. I've complained about the incompetence at your national public health agencies for years, but we've entered a new era where data and the scientific method have been completely replaced by political maneuvering. God help us all when a much more deadly pandemic arrives on our shores.

SIX

BEWARE THE TRUE BELIEVERS

L ast year, I published a book called *Stop Mass Hysteria*. I was trying to warn you about the left when I wrote, "Hatred is in the air. We're living in an age of hate in which mental pollution is worse than air pollution. The most accessible and comprehensive of all unifying agents, hatred is spreading like a virus into all too willing hosts." At the time I was referencing the left's hatred of conservatives, their hatred of Trump, and their hatred of Trump voters as examples of mass hysteria infecting America and American society.

I warned you about this, too, in my number one *New York Times* bestseller, *Trump's War*. When everyone was celebrating the election victory, I was already looking ahead. I knew what Trump was up against—what we were up against—in getting any of our agenda done. Was I right? But besides the Deep State, the Washington, D.C., Swamp, the Democrats, the RINOs, the war machine, and the fake scientists, I warned you about something else. I wrote, "Beware the true believers."

I told you about a book that made a big impact on me called *The True Believer: Thoughts on the Nature of Mass Movements*, by Eric Hoffer. It was about how people can be so consumed by one idea that they become intolerant fanatics. I could see this happening in the conservative movement. People had waited so long for a presidential candidate to run on their platform that when Donald Trump finally did it and won, they lost all sense of proportion. Nothing he said or did could be criticized, as if he were more than human.

Today, we are threatened by the fanaticism of true believers on the left and the right. Some call this "tribalism," but I believe Hoffer had it pegged more accurately. Because in the end, it all comes down to what these people believe and the extent to which they are willing to question assertions they want to believe. For a large percentage of the population, regardless of political orientation, they've lost the desire or the ability or both to do so.

For more than twenty-five years I have pointed out the hatred and stupidity of the left. I have ridiculed them. I have savaged them. I have shown you who they are. But one day, not long after the coronavirus insanity began, I woke up and realized that we have the same type of mass hysteria on the right.

WHEN PUBLIC RELATIONS TRUMPS PUBLIC HEALTH

"You know, the media, ladies and gentlemen, as you well know, is needed by you and by me, by the public—very badly needed—to be and to remain a thorn in the side of the government. In order to keep the government relatively honest, you need a media that is constantly poking at them. However, when the media instead becomes a thorn in the side of the skeptical private citizen, the media then becomes an arm of the government. Beware the government-media complex."

I spoke those words more than twenty years ago at a speech at the Commonwealth Club in San Francisco. One of the other points I made was this problem was not just a problem of the left. It transcends politics or race. The far too cozy relationship between the government and the media is a problem no matter who is in power and is a threat to the truth itself.

I wish I could tell you my warning is only of historical interest, but unfortunately that's not the case. It wasn't just the media uncritically running Nancy Pelosi's public relations visit to Chinatown here in San Francisco in late February to try to assure people there was nothing to worry about regarding the coronavirus.[1] It was also a lot of know-nothing, fake conservatives telling people there was nothing to worry about.

We used to hear about talking points coming down from the White House to the media when Obama was in office and we mocked it. Well, I'm sorry to tell you, the problem didn't go away with Obama, just as it did not go away with Clinton after I made that speech in 1998. When you hear Nancy Pelosi and once-credible conservatives saying the same thing, then you know why I said to beware the government-media complex.

To politicize a genuine public health crisis by saying the Democrats were exaggerating the risk to hurt the economy and therefore Donald Trump politically was one of the most irresponsible things I ever heard during my decades-long career in radio. But there they were, Conservative Inc. en masse, including some prominent members of the supposedly conservative media, saying exactly that.

I suppose we shouldn't be surprised because we have two motivations here. First, the Republican Party and its media mouthpieces are just as tied up with big business as the Democrat Party and its mouthpieces. And reasonable precautions against this potentially catastrophic pandemic are not good for business. That's why Mr. Dow has been feeling as poorly as many of the coronavirus patients, despite the strongest economy we've had in decades. That's number one.

Number two, those not wholly owned by the multinational corporations may have believed they were supporting Donald Trump by downplaying the pandemic and, hopefully, mitigating its effect on the economy. Everyone knows a slow economy is bad for the reelection prospects of a sitting president. So, they hoped to keep people from cutting back on economic activity by minimizing the danger from this virus.

Well, at the risk of no more desserts at the White House Hanukkah party, I'm going to tell you the truth. This has been a potentially very dangerous pandemic that needed to be taken seriously and dealt with, although not in the way left-wing governors chose to do so. By the time you read this book, the summer weather may have temporarily ended it, but it may very well return in September. Is it the end of the world? No. Is it as fatal as Ebola or SARS? No. That doesn't mean it shouldn't be taken seriously.

Even those who believe they're helping President Trump by downplaying it or encouraging him to downplay it in the media are doing him no favors. I don't know who the president's advisors were early on regarding this particular issue, but if they told him to say the coronavirus represented no danger, no threat, or that it was just media hype, they were not doing him a service. They were doing him a grave disservice. That their underreaction may have been eclipsed later by the massive overreaction does not excuse this. There was always a scientifically correct response to this virus, although it wasn't the politically correct one: selective quarantine.

DID CHINA DO THIS TO THE WORLD INTENTIONALLY?

At the outset of the pandemic, it was speculated by some panicky extremists that the government of China had created this virus in a biowarfare lab and released it upon the world on purpose. I immediately rejected this stupid thesis. Common logic dictates that the Chinese government would not infect their own people. Yet, the crazies persisted and came up with the crackpot theory that China had so much larger a population than the United States that they would be willing to sacrifice up to 200 million of their own people to cripple America.

Number one, this is patently insane. Number two, it is factually wrong and can be readily debunked. I spoke to a world-famous virologist on this subject who told me, "Of course, you're right." He said the first thing in that scenario they would have done is vaccinate their military. But they didn't vaccinate their military because there was no vaccine. So, even if it did come out of a bio lab, which he thought was very likely, it was released by accident.

No, China did not deliberately sicken the world. That makes no sense. Why would President Xi cripple China's economy and start internal unrest? The idiotic xenophobia that has been circulating on the right is shocking. It's one more sign that this country will never be the same again. Long after the virus has been suppressed and forgotten, the impact of what happened as a result of it will still be felt.

And now I see the true believers, the Trump followers vainly who want to believe that China did it on purpose. This is the new norm for the true believers, the true believers who want to blame somebody because they don't want the blame to fall upon the government itself. They do not want the blame to fall domestically. They're looking for an enemy to blame it on, and that enemy is conveniently China.

There were times during this past year where I wanted to take people by the scruff of the neck and ask, "Do you have any idea what you are saying or how stupid you sound? Do you have any idea what this will lead to? Why would China deliberately sicken the world, starting with their own country? Why would Xi cripple China's economy? Why would he risk stirring internal unrest? Do you understand you're falling into the idiotic xenophobia you've been accused of?"

Too many on the right started sounding like the right-wing goon strawmen the left is so fond of setting on fire. Some clown wrote an article that was eventually on the Drudge Report called, "Did Xi Jinping Deliberately Sicken the World?"[2] It was picked up by the self-imagined genius on right-wing radio who encouraged the gullible to believe China did do it intentionally. And I said, God, what is this man doing? What does he want to leave the world with? What legacy does he want to leave?

First, he confused true believers about the virus and told them it was nothing. It was all constructed to get Trump. And they believed him. Then they believed the stay-at-home orders were all over nothing, that everybody was out to get Trump, that it was not about the virus. Then they shifted again to blaming China because of one article. This mindless jingoism has put us in a very, very dangerous place.

No, China did not deliberately sicken the world; it would make no sense. Why would Xi cripple his own economy and stir internal unrest? We're the number one market for Chinese goods. We keep hearing about underlying conditions that are responsible for the death of so many people who contract the Covid-19 virus. Well, one of the chief underlying conditions, unfortunately of many people who declare themselves to be patriots, Americans, MAGA Trump supporters, etc., unfortunately, is xenophobia. They want to blame foreigners for everything wrong in this country.

I had to go on the air just as this right-wing hysteria was emerging to challenge all the left-wing hysteria going on at the same time. I wasn't sure I wanted to go on. To be honest, I don't know how many more shows I have left in me. I don't know how many more shows I want to do. I don't know how many shows there are *left* to do. I know that the radio industry itself is in free fall, as are most media outlets. Movies, radio, television, free fall. They're rerunning baseball games from fourteen years ago. We all know ad revenue has crippled the media.

So, I get up every day not for the money, but for one reason only: for America. I had an epiphany before the show that day. Before the show, I meditated and God spoke to me. You can laugh; it may be cynical; I don't really care. What would you call a higher sense of reasoning? I call it God speaking to us. And God spoke to me. He said, be a rabbi, not a rabble-rouser. Don't become the others. Lead them out of darkness if you can.

The word *rabbi* means teacher. I've always been a teacher, all the way back to when I was merely a teacher. And I don't say merely in a derogatory sense. I mean that in terms of where I am today. Instead of teaching with a chalkboard and giving tests, I teach through the airwaves and through my books. I told my listeners that day just what I'll say to you reading this book: Think before you speak. Think about the validity and the consequences of what you're about to say.

Yes, you're free to speak your mind but don't kid yourselves that words don't have consequences. That's why you want to make sure your words are really coming from your mind and not somewhere lower that might not produce much wisdom. They say talk is cheap, but the consequences can be expensive. So, if you join in with the mob screaming China did this on purpose, what do you propose to do about it? Are you calling for a nuclear war? Anyone who wants war with nuclear-armed China should just go down to a recruiting station and enlist, all these keyboard warriors. Let them enlist in the military.

On second thought, no, they shouldn't. First, it's not going to help the rest of us that the keyboard warriors got themselves killed when we're all reduced to ashes with them, along with millions of Chinese. And we certainly don't need more stupid people in the military. Donald Trump just spent four years trying to weed them out, while remaking the military back into a military, after eight years of Obama trying to transform it into a social engineering program.

Now, having said China did not deliberately sicken the world, I will repeat what I said from early in the crisis. It looks to me as if China was working on a biowarfare agent with viruses and this one escaped the laboratory by accident. But, you know, they're not the only country with biowarfare laboratories; the last I checked, we still have a few.

Every Western nation has biowarfare laboratories. Canada has them. The United States has them. Every big country has them. Man is a beast. Mankind is a curse on the planet. Mankind has decimated the animal life, destroyed the plant life, the air, the water, and places. And man is demonic in his desire to destroy his fellow man. China is not alone in that.

If we keep going down this road, we're going to find ourselves right where we did at the beginning of the last century, with the civilized world poised to destroy itself. We must preserve our ability to use reason and logic instead of just goose-stepping along with the jingoistic mob. They believe they know everything because they hate someone. The true believer needs someone to hate. I know this may not be what you want to hear but you must avoid becoming your own worst enemy.

I've been behind nationalism for many years. But the psychopathic nationalism of the type that Hitler stirred up is not what I've been behind. You know, there are fundamental differences between the fanatical nationalism of the fascists and the reasonable nationalism I have espoused. The chief difference is the relationship between the individual and the nation.

Hitler, Mussolini, and the rest of the fascists believed the individual was subordinate to the state. They were collectivists. They were leftists. Need I remind you that Nazi is just an abbreviation of "national *socialism*"?

That's why I've always said the left is made up of cryptofascists. They may not all be as bad as a Hitler, but their thinking is rooted in the same collectivist ideology. That's why they never talk about rights without a modifier. "Gay rights," "women's rights," "transgender rights"—there is always a modifier because they don't believe *individuals* have rights. It's a foreign concept to them. There are only group rights, themselves all subordinate to the ultimate group—the nation-state.

The nationalism I espouse is completely the opposite. The nation exists to protect the rights of the individuals who inhabit it. That is the essence of borders, language, and culture. We have strong borders to create a place where our culture and its traditions of free speech, free enterprise, and the right to pursue one's individual happiness, whatever that might be, are preserved. As I've said many times, not all cultures are equal. It's not politically correct but it's true. If it weren't, people from every Third World backwater wouldn't be desperately trying to get into this country.

It's not just about national wealth. That's putting the egg before the chicken, so to speak. Their countries are poor because they are not free. And they are not free because their cultures have not made freedom a priority. Our American culture, rooted in English common law, took more than a millennium to become what it is today. Eight hundred years ago, English barons had to pressure the king to sign Magna Carta just to establish that the king had to follow the law and not rule by his arbitrary will alone. Then followed hundreds of years more of bloody civil wars and mundane trial and error to establish the legal principles we take for granted: the right to free speech, freedom of religion, to keep and bear arms, to be free of unreasonable searches and seizures, and to a jury of one's peers if accused of a crime.

It was within the British-American cultural tradition that capitalism as we know it was born, firmly establishing property rights, the right to enter and compete in free markets, to keep the fruits of one's labor and dispose of them as one sees fit. Nowhere else on earth were the principles developed as purely and pristinely as they were in America. Americans are born and raised immersed in them, even after one hundred years of progressive war on them.

I want immigration controlled because people do not assimilate into our culture just by crossing over our borders. Some do. Some enlightened foreigners realize their countries are oppressive hellholes and yearn not only for a more comfortable situation, but for the freedom America offers to allow them to pursue their dreams. But they are the exception rather than the rule. More often, people bring their culture with them. Just look at Little Mogadishu in Minnesota and who they elected to Congress.

Like too many Americans these days, people from authoritarian cultures don't understand that our material wealth is not some magical phenomenon that just randomly occurred, but rather the result of our free, capitalist system. In the socialist hellholes they are fleeing, the dictator and his cronies are the only people who are wealthy and they acquired their wealth illegitimately. So, they assume anyone wealthy here acquired his or her wealth illegitimately. So, they vote Democrat, against the evil rich, or so they think. Having been born and raised in an authoritarian society that only a socialist revolution can address, they instinctively assume the same conditions here until they've had time to adjust. Sometimes the parents never assimilate and only their children do. That's why we can't continue to allow tens of millions of people to move within our borders unchecked. Most of the world is authoritarian and poor. If we simply transfer their populations here, we'll become them instead of them becoming us.

Well, let me tell you what else is typical of collectivist thinking: jingoism. The demonization of "the other." The war cry in this country always began on the left until very recently. It's not that conservatism is dovish or timid or pacifist. On the contrary, conservatives seek to fight wars to win when they must be fought. But true conservatives are always reluctant to go to war. War is a tragedy no matter who wins. It should always be a last resort. Conservatives believe a nation should go to war after careful consideration and elimination of all other alternatives. That is because they know they are risking the sovereignty of the nation that protects the rights of the individuals who inhabit it.

The left is always eager for war. They are the ones who got us into all the big ones, until the idiot George W. Bush came along. For them, the war is only about the glory of the collective. When you hear the jingoistic cries of belligerence, that is the sound of an unruly mob. Demonizing enemies of the state is common to all the socialist dictatorships of the twentieth century and it's no different today. Even when self-professed conservatives do it, it's a left-wing instinct. It's what Hitler did. It's what Stalin did. It's what Mao did. It's what conservatives never do.

There's enough fanaticism in the world among fanatical Islamists. We don't need to emulate them by demonizing China the way they demonize Christians and Jews.

This is what we're seeing now. This is a product of years and years of brainwashing on the right to make them think like leftists when it comes to foreign relations. The neoconservatives have done their job well since infiltrating the conservative movement after leaving the Democrat Party. And they're all over Twitter, the sewer pipe of the mind. I've never seen hatred quite like it and I've seen a lot.

I believe, but don't know for sure, that this virus was created in a Chinese lab. I believe it escaped by accident. And I know they tried to cover it up afterward. None of that is the same thing as saying they did it on purpose. Until there is irrefutable proof, and let's hope that proof never comes, we shouldn't be making that accusation. Nothing but war can come of it.

As I said on my show at the time, the whole is greater than the sum of its parts. I was quoting Aristotle, someone you probably didn't get when you were reading the sports pages and following your favorite team. Yes, I'm being arrogant, I'm being supercilious, I'm being condescending because I've had enough of this crap. I've had enough of lowbrow morons on Twitter thinking that they're equal to the greatest minds of our time because they can write six words.

So, what did Aristotle mean by "The whole is greater than the sum of its parts"? Well, I gave you an example. I said,

you have a small-minded man like Anthony Fauci, a failure from the get-go. A little delivery boy in a pharmacy in
Brooklyn, he wound up in the National Institutes of Health
(NIH) and stayed there for forty years because of his connections to the Clinton Foundation and the rest of the Democrat
Party machine. This so-called scientist quotes two statistics
in a vacuum and bases opinions about policies that will affect
all of society upon them. He was looking only at the part of
the puzzle represented by projections, statistics, and the incidence of disease without looking at the overall whole, which
is the whole economy, the whole society. The whole is greater
than the sum of its parts.

Just as we shouldn't allow narrow-minded bureaucrats
to make decisions that affect all of society, we also shouldn't
allow ourselves to be panicked or stampeded into risking
war with China because of one article that was written by
some unknown jerk. We have a substantial fight ahead of us
against the radical left who are running full speed ahead with
their own lies and idiotic conspiracy theories, backed up with
funded and organized violence and destruction in our streets.
We need to ensure our response is based in facts and reason
and not succumb to the same mindless acceptance of anything prominent people in our own movement might say for
their own reasons.

"Question with boldness even the existence of a god,"
wrote Thomas Jefferson to his young nephew Peter Carr.[3] If
Jefferson was willing to go that far, we can at least question
the assertions of prominent conservatives when they are of
dubious logic or factuality.

SEVEN

THE WAR ON OUR LIBERTY

THE AMERICAN SHUTDOWN

They didn't just close our bars and restaurants. They didn't just ban us from traveling by air. The liberal maniacs running San Francisco and several Bay Area counties, including my own, locked us down in our homes, forbidden to leave except under limited circumstances.[1]

That's where it started, with New York soon to follow. It's no coincidence that the most liberal governors of the most liberal states were the first to impose these draconian measures.

If a foreign power wanted to take over the country and knew they could do so by scaring Americans to death with a virus that is not as lethal as these Democrat governors told us it was, they couldn't do a better job. These lockdowns Governors Newsom and Cuomo pioneered are nothing more than a power grab. They used projected deaths and morbidity of the coronavirus using faulty methodology as their excuse to impose what amounts to martial law—euphemized as "social distancing"—on a population that was sadly too willing to comply.

It's a sad day when South Korea is a freer country than the "land of the free," but I'm afraid that day has come. South Korea did a wonderful job curbing the spread of the virus without imposing the draconian measures so many states in this union have imposed. The South Koreans didn't shut anything down. While Americans were cowering in their homes, South Koreans were still going to work.

"South Korea is a democratic republic, we feel a lockdown is not a reasonable choice," said Kim Woo-Joo, an infectious disease specialist at Korea University.[2] Gee, I thought the United States of America was a democratic republic. That's what they told me when I went to school.

That's not to say the South Koreans did nothing. They did quite a bit of the right things, like testing everybody. Instead of quarantining the entire nation—previously the stuff of dystopian fiction—they quarantined just those who needed to be quarantined. That's what should have been done in this country. We should quarantine those who test positive and the vulnerable communities who are at higher risk than the general population.

There is absolutely no reason nor precedent for what happened to our country during the initial outbreak of this virus. It's a power grab, pure and simple. They immediately rush to nationalize, to centralize, and to take control of your life. None of it makes sense. We're looking at an economic debacle in our nation that we haven't seen in our lifetimes—perhaps in U.S. history. But the damage to our liberty is even more dangerous than that.

This used to be a nation based on the "most good for the most people." That's what they told me when I was growing up. Yet, New York governor Andrew Cuomo had the nerve to say that if he saved just one life by locking down the entire state, it would be worth it to him.

Do you realize how insane that is?

This is the same governor who says killing millions of unborn children is an essential right of women. He's full of crap. It's not about saving one life. It's about controlling millions of lives, which is all these demagogues have ever dreamed of.

I would never have believed that so many people would have given up so many of their rights so quickly, without so much as a whimper. Nobody in California said to Governor Newsom, "Wait, not so fast." No one has said, "Wait a minute, you have no right to tell me I can't leave my house without your permission. Who in hell do you think you are?"

He even publicly toyed with the idea of imposing martial law. I live in the San Francisco area. The government had the entire area in lockdown. Everyone was in fear. All these Bay Area liberals who make believe they're so wild and free are scared little rabbits hunkering down in their burrows because someone in the government said, "Don't move."

Newsom read one Johns Hopkins projection, from one epidemiological study, on one computer program, and from that alone he became Mussolini. Isn't it odd that a man who poses as a "liberal" takes away our freedoms like this? Am I the only one who finds all of this rather strange?

At some point, there is going to be a reaction to this insanity in this nation. At some point, people will rebel against this lockdown. Or will I be the lone voice dissenting to this madness? It wouldn't be the first time.

This destruction of our liberty by two "liberal" governors who think they're going to be president someday because they released their inner Mussolinis was no surprise to me.

Let me explain something to you. If we are that willing to give up all our rights over this illness, what happens when this virus passes? What if we get a demagogue in power who says, "Because (fill in the blank), I want you to do X, Y, and Z"? Maybe he will want you to give up your guns.

Mayor Latoya Cantrell of New Orleans already pulled that, using the coronavirus as her excuse. More specifically, she invoked the emergency power to allow the superintendents of the fire and police departments to ban the sale or transport of firearms, alcohol, explosives, or combustibles.[3]

This isn't the first time a mayor of New Orleans has done this. Mayor Ray Nagin did the same thing during the state of emergency related to Hurricane Katrina. He went even farther; he had the police pounding on doors and seizing guns from private owners who weren't trying to sell or transport them at all. One of the same pro–Second Amendment groups who sued the city back then is already threatening to sue it again.[4]

This didn't just happen in New Orleans. Mayor Deborah Frank Feinen of Champaign, Illinois, did the same thing even though her town hadn't affirmed a single case of the disease when she issued the proclamation.[5] Her proclamation covered imposing curfews, banning alcohol sales, fixing prices, closing businesses, and a host of other tyrannical measures. That one got some pushback from conservative media and the mayor issued a clarification stating the city would not be banning gun or alcohol sales or seizing property—at least not yet.[6]

By the way, Feinen is a Republican, although likely of the RINO variety.

I had firsthand experience with the assault on our right to keep and bear arms. I went to a sporting goods store to buy ammunition while all this was going on. No, I wasn't stocking up on ammo to defend my hoarded toilet paper. I need the ammunition for the range because I have to requalify for a certain license I have. I had to buy fifty rounds of several calibers.

I called the store and the clerk said, "Yeah, we have .380, we have .357, we have .45, have shotgun shells," etc. I asked if they had enough for what I needed and the clerk said they did. So I went to the store.

When I got there, there was a man from across the Bay in front of me in line. He steps right up, they check his name, and he walks out with bags of ammunition. When it was my turn, the clerk asked for my ID and I gave him my California driver's license.

"That's not valid," said the clerk. He told me my license was "federally restricted," and was not a qualified license. "Why didn't you tell me that on the phone before I drove all the way down here?" I asked. "I don't know; you didn't ask," he replied.

I suppose I walked into that one.

Eventually, he told me I had to provide both my passport and valid license so my information could be sent to the fascist goons in Sacramento for them to decide whether I'll be permitted to buy ammunition. This is the world we're living in now. They had already nullified the Second Amendment through this bureaucratic mumbo jumbo. Now they want to use the coronavirus to repeal it completely.

Of course, the liberal war on the Bill of Rights isn't limited to the Second Amendment. Governor Ralph "Blackface" Northam used the crisis to step up his own assault on the First Amendment by making it a criminal offense to hold a church service attended by more than ten people.[7] This was done by executive order under Virginia's state of emergency laws, which gives the governor extraordinary powers during a state of emergency.[8] Without opening the whole can of worms as to whether the First Amendment to the U.S. Constitution applies to this state law or not—liberals generally like to invoke the Fourteenth Amendment to say the Bill of Rights applies the states when it suits their purposes and forget all about that when it doesn't—Virginia has its own constitutional protection of religious worship in its state constitution. It begins, "That religion or the duty which we owe to our Creator, and the manner of discharging it, can be directed only by reason and conviction, not by force or violence; and, therefore, all men are equally entitled to the free exercise of religion, according to the dictates of conscience; and that it is the mutual duty of all to practice Christian forbearance, love, and charity towards each other."[9]

Does Northam's executive order violate the state constitution's protection of the free exercise of religion? We'll have to see if it is challenged in court. That's not to say judges always get decisions right. Too often, they come down on the side of the government. No system is perfect. We shouldn't be surprised that allowing the government itself to be the judge of its own powers often results in them discovering new ones.

"LIBERAL" GOVERNORS?

If there is one thing we've learned from the Covid-19 crisis, it's the amount of power we've ceded to our state governments. I'm not sure if most Americans are aware of how open-ended their state constitutions are. The U.S. Constitution is framed with the understanding that the federal government has only the powers delegated to it in the Constitution, all others being left to the states or the people. Does the federal government routinely exceed those enumerated powers? Of course, but at least on paper it is supposed to be limited to what is delegated.

The U.S. Bill of Rights is only understood to emphasize and protect some very important rights. Those ten amendments do not represent the only limits on the federal government's power. The government is supposed to be prohibited from exercising *any* power not specifically delegated to it.

The state constitutions, however, are framed on a completely opposite premise. They are written to assume the state legislature can make any law it wants, as long as the law doesn't violate a right protected by the state constitution's bill of rights. That's an enormous opportunity for power at the state level that we may want to rethink. For now, however, state constitutions allow for these emergency powers, including the closing of businesses, banning firearms sales, commandeering of private property, suspension of laws limiting executive power, and all sorts of other draconian measures.

As just one example, New York State's Executive Law Article 2-B gives its governor the following powers in a state of emergency:

a. the establishment of a curfew and the prohibition and control of pedestrian and vehicular traffic, except essential emergency vehicles and personnel;
b. the designation of specific zones within which the occupancy and use of buildings and the ingress and egress of vehicles and persons may be prohibited or regulated;
c. the regulation and closing of places of amusement and assembly;
d. the suspension or limitation of the sale, dispensing, use or transportation of alcoholic beverages, firearms, explosives, and flammable materials and liquids;
e. the prohibition and control of the presence of persons on public streets and places;[10]

This list of emergency powers goes on after that, but I think you get the picture. We've quietly allowed state governors the power to impose what amounts to martial law over us just by saying the magic words, "state of emergency." Perhaps the silver lining here will be people reexamining these powers and how they could be used in the future. Don't think for a minute this is the last time this will happen. If history is any judge, powers acquired during an emergency become routine once the government gets away with exercising them the first time.

The bad news is that every state has an emergency powers act that somewhat resembles New York's. California's is the

California Emergency Services Act. But notice which state governors were the ones to use them first and most extensively. It was all the so-called liberal governors. Newsom in California, Cuomo in New York, and old Blackface in Virginia led the charge. As of this writing, fifteen states had imposed similar lockdowns on their populations, almost all of them liberal "blue states."[11]

Doesn't it strike you as odd that the supposed "liberals" are the ones adopting the most draconian measures, driving the economy into a possible depression and their people into prison cells? As I said on my radio show and in the public health chapter of this book, this virus must be taken seriously and reasonable precautions must be employed, but what governors like Cuomo and Newsom did were unnecessary and intolerable in terms of their harm to civil liberties.

This is the face of fascism. How long have I told you the people who call themselves liberals are the real fascists? They always have been. They want nothing but unchecked, unquestioned, raw power. They thrive on crises like this, not because they want to serve the public, but because they want to rule the public. And they know the public is vulnerable to ceding some of their liberty during an alarming crisis. It's happened so many times throughout history that it's astonishing people don't see it coming from a mile away. But then again, nobody educated in our public schools knows any history.

What does the word "liberal" mean? Well, the definition has certainly evolved over time. It comes from the Latin word "liberalus," meaning "suitable for a freeman," according to Merriam-Webster's dictionary.[12] Even in this country, liberal at one time meant you favored individual liberty, laissez-faire free markets, and limited government. Now they call those people conservatives or libertarians.

But even when I was growing up in a Democrat household, liberal still had a connection to the idea of liberty. Liberals at that time may have given up on economic liberty, but they were still strong supporters of civil liberties. The liberals of my father's generation would never have stood for what Cuomo or Newsom did to their states because they would have recognized it immediately for what it was: fascism. My father's generation were the people who fought a long, bloody war against the fascists.

Today, there is no connection left between modern American liberals and the idea of liberty. Bill de Blasio, the known communist, called for the nationalization of medical supply companies.[13] Sean Penn, the stoned maniac, suddenly pops up out of the woodwork of a pot high and also wants nationalization, although he wants to call in the military.[14]

Let's remember who Sean Penn is. He is the man who went to Cuba and Venezuela to glorify socialist authoritarianism in those countries.[15] He's the man who interviewed El Chapo and said he regretted his interview failed "to start a conversation about the war on drugs" when this drug lord with the blood of thousands on his hands was arrested a week later.[16] Now, suddenly, he's an expert on how civil society should work?

Let me remind you of something. Nationalizing industries, including medical supplies, is what they did in Venezuela. How did that work out for Venezuelans? This is what they did in the Soviet Union. How did it work out there for the Russians? They tried it in Cuba. How are they doing with the nationalization of health care there? They can hardly manu-facture anything in Cuba, least of all medical supplies. They don't make any medications; there are no discoveries there.

Yet, liberals never learn, no matter how many times the failure of their ideas is demonstrated. The conservative econ-omist Thomas Sowell once said, "The most fundamental fact about the ideas of the political left is that they do not work. Therefore we should not be surprised to find the left concen-trated in institutions where ideas do not have to work in order to survive." But here they are again, trying to implement ideas that have failed before and are still failing elsewhere in real time.

They don't care. Success is not their goal; their goal is power. The truth is today's liberals are using the virus as an excuse to try to get what they've always wanted but didn't think they could get away with. These people are not your friends. They are cryptofascists and they must be stopped.

FREEDOM FOR BUMS AND CRIMINALS ONLY

As tyrannical as their designs on most of us may be, though, there are some people liberals want to give total freedom. Who are they? I posted an answer on Twitter back in March. It said,

> Why is SAN FRAN area in LOCKDOWN? 3 principle reasons; 1) largest CHINESE POPULATION outside of China (many are undocumented-may have recently traveled there); 2) huge HOMELESS population; 3) IMMUNE-COMPROMISED hiv population . . . am I wrong?[17]

A Chinese friend of mine, a doctor, agreed with me on the Chinese population. We don't even know who is in our city, much less whether they have recently traveled back to China. They go back and forth all the time.

Then there are the bums. Government vermin locking us down in our homes doesn't do anything about the virus spreading among the homeless population. How long have I been telling my listeners we have to get them off the streets? And of course, we have a large population of people with HIV infections who would be at increased risk of serious illness or death from the disease.

I'm surprised my tweet is still published on Twitter; it says so many forbidden things. How do you know they are forbidden? Well, they're all true. That's the first clue. As Orwell said, "Truth is treason in an empire of lies." But that's a subject for another chapter.

Under liberalism, they let the bums and illegal aliens live but let the taxpayers die. I know that sounds over-the-top until you consider just how the bums—"the homeless," in liberal speak—were treated during the Covid-19 lockdowns. Not only were they put up in hotels at taxpayer expense, they were given alcohol and drugs, including marijuana and methadone by the San Francisco Department of Public Health (SFDPH).[18] I've said many times that this country should reopen the state mental institutions and involuntarily admit the "homeless" population so they can get the mental health treatment they need. The San Francisco public health officials giving them free drugs and alcohol, on the other hand, should be arrested and thrown in jail.

I doubt that will happen as long as the city is run by London Breed, San Francisco's invented mayor. But how much will finally be too much? SFDPH claimed the drugs and alcohol aren't at taxpayer expense in a tweet chock full of some of the most impressive doublespeak I've heard in years.

> These harm reduction based practices, which are not unique to San Francisco, and are not paid for with taxpayer money, help guests successfully complete isolation and quarantine and have significant individual and public health benefits in the COVID-19 pandemic.[19]

Guests? They're calling the bums guests. They're supposed to be providing them treatment, so if "bums" is too politically incorrect then at the very least call them "patients." No, to these criminals the bums are guests. And I'd like to know where the money is coming from if it isn't coming from taxpayers. At the very least it's being distributed by public health employees being paid by taxpayers. Where are they getting the drugs and alcohol? You tell me. I haven't a clue.

So, small businesses are closing all over California because they can't get a dime from the government after being ordered to close down, but San Francisco's bums have free drugs. This is a city that is so insane that no one who doesn't live here can possibly understand. Then again, the whole nation gets a pretty good idea every time Nancy Pelosi opens her mouth.

The FBI needs to raid San Francisco and arrest the management. I'd start with the mayor and put her in prison for what she's doing. How can one psychotic mayor hold an entire city hostage? How could a whole city come to a halt because one human being said, "You must stay home"? How did Americans become so passive that they would give up their freedoms so quickly? Why have they expressed no outrage at this gigantic rip-off called the CARES Act?

I've been warning about the health risks the homeless population pose to the rest of us for a long time. Back in 2018, I wrote an article for Newsmax titled "Homeless Bring Diseases to Cities—Time to Remove Them from Streets."[20] Even by that time I had already been telling my listeners for years that once-beautiful San Francisco was filthier than Third World cities I had visited. But I was the only one at the time warning about the health risks this population represented.

It's not just unpleasant to look at a city riddled with hypodermic needles, feces, and urine. It's dangerous. Even without a potentially deadly virus going around, human feces alone can become airborne, releasing potentially dangerous viruses such as the rotavirus. These can be inhaled, end up in your intestines, and prove fatal, especially for children. That's a risk we were already living with before Covid-19.

Now, you tell me why, if it's necessary for all of society to be locked in their homes, why are these people still roaming the streets? Do you think they're practicing social distancing and washing their hands every time they touch a hard surface? There is no more ideal place for a virus to spread than among a large population living in squalor in a confined space. Yet, with liberals running San Francisco and other large metropolitan areas, these people are roaming free while responsible, hardworking people who are far more likely to take reasonable precautions are under martial law.

What do I propose to do about it? My recommendation hasn't changed in decades. Given the social safety nets we have in place, anyone choosing to live in squalor outdoors must be mentally ill. There is no other explanation for the choices these people are making. We need to get them the care they need and we can't ask them their opinion about it while they are not in control of their faculties and posing a danger to the rest of society.

Until the 1970s, vagrancy laws were commonplace in America. It used to be considered a misdemeanor to be a vagrant. Do you think that's harsh? In England, vagrants were whipped, branded, conscripted into military service, or exiled to penal colonies. That was harsh. In America they were simply fined or jailed for a short period of time.

My solution is more compassionate. We need to forcibly remove bums across America to special places built for them to get the care they need. Take them one hundred miles or so outside of city centers to facilities built just for them and give them rehabilitation. If they can't be rehabilitated, reopen the mental hospitals and put those who can't be rehabilitated into the mental hospitals where they can get the care that they need.

Yes, I've heard all the conspiracy theories that the epidemic was a hoax by the Democrats or others for the purpose of bringing down the Trump administration. I've argued against that since early on and elsewhere in this book. Obviously, it's a real virus that can be very deadly. But the more we learned about the virus together, the more we realized that it's not deadly for everyone. It didn't hit all cities and counties with the same severity. Early on when Dr. Slouchy was still telling you the coronavirus was nothing to worry about, I was the only one calling for selective quarantine.

I listed the groups that should have been quarantined while the rest of us were allowed to go about our business. I studied epidemiology, but you don't have to be a genius or an epidemiologist to understand the basics of how epidemics work. You don't isolate a whole city. You isolate those communities most at risk. The elderly and people with underlying medical conditions or otherwise compromised immune systems are the people for whom this virus represents a danger. They are the only ones who should have been sheltered in place.

Is this a perfect solution? No. We don't live in a perfect world. It's the best solution anyone has proposed so far. Or do you believe mentally ill vagrants roaming freely, spreading disease, while healthy Americans are forbidden even to go to work is a better solution?

If you're like me and think that's crazy, it's nothing compared to what liberals are suggesting for criminals. We can debate all day about whether it's "just" to confine mentally ill people against their will. But we've really gone off the deep end when we decide we should no longer confine criminals against their will. But that's just what the mentally ill people who have homes—liberals—have been doing since the Covid-19 pandemic started.

I probably don't have to tell you which cities and states led this charge. Among the first was that same naked communist who wanted to nationalize the medical supplies industry,

Mayor Bill de Blasio of New York City. As of this writing, de Blasio planned to loose more than one thousand convicts onto the streets of the tri-state area around New York City.[21] He was releasing them for their own protection from prisoners with Covid-19, which included Harvey Weinstein. You'd think the convicts would know enough to steer clear of Weinstein already.

Not to be outdone, failed presidential candidate Kamala Harris introduced a bill in the U.S. Senate to release thousands of federal prisoners "in California, and around the United States" into community supervision.[22] Her fellow failed presidential candidate and liberal senator Cory Booker cosponsored the bill.

As of this writing, four states were considering the mass release of criminals from jail to protect them from Covid-19.[23] This policy had the full support of *Jacobin* magazine, which should tell you all you need to know about its wisdom.[24]

Then there were the criminals who weren't in prison yet, even though they should have been. People were sending me pictures while the shelter-in-place orders were in effect showing MS-13 and other violent drug gangs who weren't practicing "social distancing." You didn't see these pictures in any newspapers because we don't have real newspapers anymore. We don't have an independent media anymore.

These gang members were congregating, sitting in cars, smoking, and drinking beer, while the police did nothing. The police are afraid of them, but they're not afraid of white people driving around in SUVs in the suburbs. They certainly weren't afraid of a solitary white surfer who was arrested for paddleboarding alone in the ocean.[25]

I know that sounds like I got it off a satire website, but I didn't. These liberal fascists actually broke the social distancing guidelines to put handcuffs on a man who had presumably left his house alone, drove to the ocean alone in his automobile, and paddleboarded on the ocean alone. There was zero chance of this man infecting anyone or anyone infecting him until the police put their hands on him!

This just emphasizes my point more. For the cryptofascist liberals, this is not primarily about public health. It's about control. The paddleboarder endangered no one, but he failed the primary "liberal" test. He didn't follow orders.

So here we are. We're putting all of America on house arrest, except for vagrants and criminals, whom we're leaving alone or setting free from prison. And you wonder why I call liberalism a mental disorder?

LIFE OR LIBERTY?

It was inevitable that two schools of thought would emerge about the coronavirus. And, of course, in our hyperpoliticized culture, those two schools generally separated along political lines. One, made up mostly of Trump supporters, believed the virus was all hype. They believed it was purely social control by the politicians. It was a hyped-up seasonal flu designed to destroy the economy, ensure that Donald Trump would not be elected president, and turn America into a socialist state.

The other side believed the virus was very serious and could kill millions. They believed it should mitigate all other concerns. All our democracy should go out the window, along with all of our freedoms. Now, I'm not saying all or even most of these people consciously wanted to kill the economy just to hurt Donald Trump's reelection chances. But let's face it. If you were dead set against a second Trump term, you may have subconsciously been more open to the suggestion that this was a plague worthy of taking the record-breaking economy Trump was riding to reelection down a notch.

Does every single person fit neatly into one of those psychological profiles? No. But I've been around for a long time, seen many a political movement come and go, and I'd lay you odds one of the two described an awful lot of Americans, perhaps most Americans.

Which group did I fall into? As usual, neither. One night, while this hysteria on both sides was near its apex, I lay awake all night trying to remember where I had last put a journal article I've saved for about forty years now, about sorcery, illness, and social control in a Philippine municipality.

The next day, I went to my library, which is in another house. And lo and behold, I found it. It was from the *Southwestern Journal of Anthropology,* Summer 1960.[26] I went looking for this and some old articles about epidemiology to reconnect with my previous work. I wanted to bring my background to the foreground.

We're living in a virtual police state, without so much as an argument in Congress or any state legislature about how far the powers of the police should go, or could go, or will go. There hasn't been one word of opposition raised by a single First Amendment attorney saying, "Wait a minute. Where did the police acquire that power? When did they acquire that power?"

These are questions that I thought would have been asked by now.

THE FASCIST RESPONSE TO A REAL THREAT

So, why was a one-size-fits-all approach implemented by these demonic, maniac, left-wing governors? Why didn't the so-called press question any of these very questionable tactics? It's because there is a conspiracy, not of dunces, but of very evil people. The virus itself wasn't a hoax, but the idea that locking down all of society, rather than just the vulnerable, was the only or even an effective way of dealing with the virus *was* a hoax. And the only way we're going to break the chains of this hoax is to start going about our business regardless of the insane edicts of a few liberal dictators.

The Coronavirus Catastrophe showed us the cryptofascism that's been lying just under the surface all along. We saw cops body slamming a woman in an Alabama Walmart for refusing to wear a mask.[27] And when I say "body slammed," I'm not exaggerating. Video of the incident shows the officer reaching between the legs of the woman while trying to handcuff her, lifting her completely off the ground, and hurling her down on the hard floor, headfirst. When her friends objected, it appeared the cops maced them. In New York City, a cop threatened a man with a stun gun, threw him to the sidewalk, and kneeled on his back for breaking social distancing laws.[28]

What self-respecting officer of the law would go along with this as if they were in the Germany of the 1930s and "just following orders"? It's not as if I'm anti-cop. I defended the cops in New York City and elsewhere when it was literally open season on them during the Obama years. And I don't have a problem with rough treatment, when necessary, to bring in a criminal who is suspected of committing a murder, an assault, a rape, or a robbery who doesn't want to come along peacefully. But a man accused of not "social distancing"? A female bar owner who opened her business to survive? At some point the cops have to push back and say, "Go to hell. I'm not arresting people for opening their restaurants." There was one thing I was sure of in early April. The indiscriminate lockdown of every business and every individual was not going to go on for long. People will tolerate their freedom being abridged for a short time during an emergency, but there is only so much social control that can be exerted over a population until it rebels.

EIGHT

THE WAR ON OUR CONSTITUTION

I've told my listeners time and again, "No president is going to give us everything we want." Donald Trump won't, but no one else who sought the White House anytime recently would have come nearly as close. I have plenty to say in another chapter about the stimulus plan the president signed, packed with pork barrel spending that would have made Franklin Delano Roosevelt blush. But make no mistake: the president's response to the coronavirus, despite some mistakes, did something far more important than contain a virus or subsidize failing businesses. It saved the Constitution.

A FEDERAL REPUBLIC IF WE CAN KEEP IT

The one bright spot in this authoritarian nightmare has been that the Cuomo or Newsom approach is not universal within our borders. As of this writing, forty-three of the fifty states had issued some form of stay-at-home or shelter-in-place

139

directives, but seven had not.[1] More important, the approach each state took was not identical, something the liberal fascists couldn't contain their hysteria over.

"Trump administration's lack of a unified coronavirus strategy will cost lives, say a dozen experts," bleated NBC News.[2] That's all so-called liberals know: unrestrained, centralized power. They still believe every Democrat they anoint to the presidency is a philosopher king who should manage every minute detail of our communities and our lives. That's why when the people sent that smooth-talking shyster Barack Obama a clear message by taking the House and Senate away from him in 2014, he responded by saying he'd simply rule with his "pen and phone."

That is fascism defined. The will of the unitary leader, à la Mussolini, is a central element of fascism. It's not the only one but it's the first and most important element everyone thinks of when they throw out the "f-word."

Donald Trump, the supposed fascist, the man the left has called "Literally Hitler," has taken the opposite approach. He's left the internal decisions up to the governors of the various states. That's the constitutional approach. He seems to understand what no one on the left or in the media understands: the president doesn't have the power to order the kinds of drastic measures state governors have ordered.

Generally, I don't go around quoting the founding fathers chapter and verse. That doesn't mean I haven't read and thought about them. One thing the founders believed was that internal matters were to be largely governed by the state governments. The federal government was there to defend the borders and referee commerce between the states and that's about it. If you don't believe me, here is what James Madison wrote in *Federalist* 45:

> The powers delegated by the proposed Constitution to the federal government are few and defined. Those which are to remain in the State governments are numerous and indefinite. The former will be exercised principally on external objects, as war, peace, negotiation, and foreign commerce; with which last the power of taxation will, for the most part, be connected.
>
> The powers reserved to the several States will extend to all the objects which, in the ordinary course of affairs, concern the lives, liberties, and properties of the people, and the internal order, improvement, and prosperity of the State.[3]

President Trump made this same point in a scathing letter to that shameless hypocrite, Chuck Schumer. "As you are aware," wrote the president, "the Federal Government is merely a back-up for state governments. Unfortunately, your state needed far more of a back-up than most others."[4]

Is the president a constitutional scholar? I doubt it. He's a businessman. He's practical and became a billionaire by doing what works, because if he didn't, he'd be out of business. Like most successful businessmen, he was out of business a few times and had to pick himself up off the ground.

Our federal system is important not because some wise men who have been dead for hundreds of years said it was. It's important because it works. It's the only system that could work in a nation this large and diverse. Now, when I say "diverse," I don't mean racially. I mean culturally. We have an American culture—despite the nonstop war upon it by the left—but we also have a plethora of subcultures in America. You don't need a PhD in anthropology to understand that Minnesota and Wisconsin are culturally different from midtown Manhattan.

Even in normal times, what works in midtown Manhattan does not work in Wisconsin. What works in Wisconsin doesn't work in rural Idaho. And what works in rural Idaho doesn't work in downtown Los Angeles or San Francisco.

During a pandemic, you can multiply that principle by ten. It still astounds me that even the cryptofascist liberals can believe that the exact same measures being taken in densely populated urban centers like New York, San Francisco, or Chicago should be taken in the mountains of Montana or Colorado. While I don't agree with the decision to lock down the healthy with the sick anywhere, at least you can understand the reasoning, however flawed, in a crowded city. But why would you want to enforce that policy on farmers, who largely work under conditions where they are far apart from each other or alone? It might actually result in more Covid-19 cases that discourage farmers from going outside for long periods of exposure to sunlight, one of the best antiviral agents known to man.

It's not just farmers who derive a benefit from sunlight against Covid-19. A study published in June found that not only can summer sunlight wipe out over 90 percent of Covid-19 virus on surfaces within thirty-four minutes, but that "healthy people outdoors receiving sunlight could have been exposed to lower viral dose with more chances for mounting an efficient immune response."[5] That suggests stay-at-home orders by the maniac governors may have done more harm than good.

In addition to being constitutional and eminently practical, the state-by-state approach also gives us the opportunity to judge the efficacy of different approaches to managing the virus, to see which is the most effective. This won't be the last worldwide pandemic or even the last epidemic in the United States. With the potential of up to fifty slightly different approaches or even a few radically different approaches, we have an opportunity to discover what we never could with one, unitary national policy.

If you're trying to figure out how liberals could possibly object to that, I'll let you in on a little secret. Actually, it's not a secret; I've been saying it for decades but it's easy to forget during times like these. Liberals don't care what's most effective. They aren't primarily interested in what works. If they were, they wouldn't insist on increasing the funding for the Department of Education every year. Liberals are interested in ruling us, period. What else could explain urban liberal media shills in New York City going apoplectic because some farmers in Montana aren't social distancing the way they want them to?

It's the same fascist instinct that drove them to impose rules on restroom signs in South Dakota, regardless of what the South Dakotans wanted. They just can't stand the idea that there may be people anywhere who don't run their local communities in the same, insane manner liberal politicians run my home city of San Francisco.

Well, after more than a month of hearing that he had failed America because he hadn't imposed a top down,

one-size-fits-all, unconstitutional policy on the whole country, the president pulled one of his classic chess moves. He
came out and announced that he would be making the decision as to when the states could allow their businesses to
reopen. "Whether we like it or not, there is a certain instinct
to it. People want to get back to work. We have to bring our
country back. So, I'll be making a decision reasonably soon,"
Trump said on April 11.[6]

Now, you would think the liberal governors and their
media minions would see how obviously the president was
baiting them. They didn't. They are so unhinged with hatred
for the president that they came out firing both barrels in
defense of the strategy the president had been pursuing all
along.

"Trump claims it's his call on when to 'reopen' the country. He's wrong," screamed a headline on NBC News.[7] Having
asked "the experts," the intrepid NBC reporters sanctimo-
niously declared that the closing of businesses is a police
power, which is reserved to the states. Of course, that's correct, which is why the president had been leaving that decision to the governors all along, while being excoriated by the
same people who now insisted the approach they criticized
was correct!

With news reporting like this, who needs satire?

Governor "Sausage and Peppers" Cuomo even trotted
out the usual liberal cry of wolf, saying, "we will have a constitutional crisis like you haven't seen in decades, where states
tell the federal government, 'We're not going to follow your
order.'"[8] The liberals have been warning of an impending
constitutional crisis for all four years of Trump's presidency,

while he's been the most faithful president to the Constitution in decades.

So, yes, the president outmaneuvered the liberals again and had them demanding he take the approach they had been criticizing literally days before. It's sad that a president must waste his time playing games like this during a pandemic but thank goodness Trump found a way to get the media behind the constitutional approach. He even had them thinking they had won a victory against him. The federal government issued recommendations and the states made the final decisions on whether to close down their economies, when to reopen them, and how.

I don't happen to agree with any of the governors who closed down their economies instead of implementing selective quarantine, but at least our constitutional system was preserved. I doubt that would have been the case under any other recent president.

OPERATION WARP SPEED?

I have four dogs, one being little Teddy, the mascot of the Savage Nation. Teddy is sixteen, largely blind and deaf, and a cancer survivor. His condition is sad in a way, but he hangs out with the other dogs and doesn't seem to know himself that anything is wrong with him. One night after dinner, I turned around with my glass of wine and there was Teddy trying to mount our two-pound teacup poodle. I said, "What are you doing, Teddy? Your chestnuts have been removed! You had cancer!"

It occurred to me at that moment that Teddy has phantom chestnuts, just as those poor people who have lost an arm or a leg feel like the missing limb is still there. They call that a "phantom arm" or a "phantom leg." So, Teddy has phantom chestnuts just like the phantom Constitution and phantom Bill of Rights we have right now.

We also have a phantom budget. It's not real. We make believe we have a budget. Pelosi and McConnell ram through bailouts, Trump signs them, and the Federal Reserve prints up the money. Fortunately, we're kept abreast of all this by the phantom media that graduated from "fake news" to "phantom news." The news has been replaced by propaganda, but many believe the news is still there.

The Democrats have even managed to field a phantom candidate. He's not even real. Like all phantoms, he is an apparition without substance, the mere shadow of a man who wasn't that bright even when he had all his marbles. Joe Biden is a hologram in a basement.

But certainly, the most frightening of all these phantoms is the phantom Constitution. I remember President Trump's speech in mid-May about his hopes for a coronavirus vaccine by the end of the year.[9] I know I'm supposed to tell you how inspiring it was, but the truth is it made me angry. "Operation Warp Speed," as the White House is calling it, involved not only the armies of bureaucrats in the NIH, CDC, and FDA, who've been wrong on virtually everything, but the military as well.

That's right, they're planning on using the military to distribute this vaccine. Trump brought out the chairman of the Joint Chiefs of Staff, Mark Milley, who expressed how excited he was for the military to "deliver the vaccine."

To that I say, "Not even in my cold, dead arm."

I don't have a phantom arm. I have a real one. And they're not putting a rush job vaccine into it while there is still blood pumping from my heart. First, do I even have to point out that any vaccine developed by a program called "Operation Warp Speed" is unlikely to either work or be safe? The vaccines we have now for the flu are only 50 percent effective, give or take 10 percent from year to year, according to the CDC.[10]

I have a less rosy view than that front organization for the pharmaceutical industry. The flu vaccine is basically a scam. Yes, the vaccine that is available during any given year can protect you from a particular strain of the influenza virus. But when they make up the flu vaccine, months in advance of the next flu season, it is difficult for them to predict exactly which strain is going to predominate in the area you're living in.

The influenza vaccine is effective against influenza B and influenza A(H1N1) viruses, but not as effective against influenza A(H3N2) viruses.[11] The drug manufacturers can only make a vaccine that represents the industry's best guess at which strain of the flu will predominate in any given year and they often guess wrong. So, I personally will never weaken my own body with a flu shot. Never. It's one of the great scams of our time, in my opinion, even though I am generally in favor of vaccines to prevent childhood disease from spreading.

When you get down to the subset of viruses called "coronaviruses," the news is even worse. We still don't have effective vaccines for SARS or MERS that are anywhere near being safe or effective enough for commercial production.[12] We may never have them. But we're supposed to believe a Covid-19 or SARS-COV-2 vaccine rushed to market at warp speed is going to be safe and effective?

I certainly don't believe it. But the more important principle here is personal liberty. I am by no means an antivaxxer, as anyone who regularly listens to my radio show knows. But it is one thing to be in favor of vaccines, to criticize those who ignorantly don't get them when they're safe and effective, and quite another to call out the military to force people to take them.

No, Trump didn't specifically say it was going to be mandatory, at least as far as the federal government is concerned. But even if the federal government doesn't mandate the vaccine, we still have the fascist Democrat state governors to contend with. Just as they've taken away our freedom of assembly, along with most of the rest of the Bill of Rights, they will take away our freedom to make this choice, too. You'll need proof you've had the vaccine—a vaccine passport, so to speak—to go to a movie or restaurant, the beach, the golf course. Who knows? They may even set up checkpoints like they had in East Germany, so the American Stasi can ask you for your "vaccine papers."

Of course, I'm giving President Trump the benefit of the doubt that he won't push for the vaccine to be mandatory. I don't know that because no one in our phantom media thought to ask this obvious question. They are virtually all Don Lemon, plus or minus ten watts. But even they had to trip over themselves to avoid asking this question.

We're all familiar by now with the Democrats' phrase, "Never let a crisis go to waste." Well, we've seen that from both parties over this past year. The Republicans have certainly used the crisis as an excuse to spend like no Democrat in history ever dared to do. It's important that we don't let them slide on that just because the Democrats might be much worse on other things. No nation can go on running the deficits we're running, financed by printed money, without consequences. That's how you end up with a phantom currency and if you think things are bad now, just wait until that day comes.

STEALING SAVAGE

Earlier this year there was an interesting article on SFGate.com titled, "The most commonly stolen book at the San Francisco Public Library may surprise you."[13] Now, you might assume that in liberal San Francisco it might be *The Audacity of the Dopes* by our former socialist president who is now terrified his party took his propaganda seriously.[14] It isn't. No, the book that most commonly goes missing in the library's twenty-eight branches is my 2006 title, *Liberalism Is a Mental Disorder.*

I'm not as surprised as one might think about this. There are a couple of reasons I can think of as to why San Franciscans would be pilfering my wisdom. The most obvious is to keep it off the library shelves. The tech giants' efforts to eliminate conservative speech from the internet are well-publicized, but there are still people who get their information the old-fashioned way: by checking a book out of the library. So, maybe there is a contingent of leftists in San Francisco who seek to silence us the old-fashioned way, by collecting our hardcover books and burning them.

What, you thought only the Nazis burned books? I'm sure that's what Jake Tapper or your friendly neighborhood public school history teacher would like you to think. But it isn't true. Totalitarians have been burning books for thousands of years. The communists in the Soviet Union put the Nazis to shame burning books. Ironically, they wouldn't even allow their captive citizens to read Plato, one of the original communists.[15]

So, banning books, even if they don't go to the trouble of burning them, is part and parcel of left-wing totalitarianism. I wouldn't be surprised if the librarians themselves are stealing my books, taking them home and making a bonfire of their own vanities. But whoever it is, there is good reason why one of my older titles would be the most stolen. These leftists don't want anyone to know I was warning people about the effects this mental disorder would have on our body politic long before we got to the cesspool we're swimming in today.

Forget America as a whole for a moment; just look at San Francisco, a once-beautiful city. It's now the human feces capital of the world. There was an article on a local television station's website late last year titled, "Call to Action: Feces Complaints Increase in San Francisco."[16] The article lamented a "35-percent increase in feces complaints from 2017 to 2018."

A 35 percent increase? Is that really the problem? Have I lost my mind, or should we be horrified there are any feces complaints at all? One of the great achievements of the industrial revolution was the elimination of human feces from the streets of our cities. Before the development of municipal sewers, human waste was deposited in outhouses and cesspools and had to be carried away by "night soil men," who mucked out the cesspools and transported the foul cargo out of the city in carts, spilling or smearing a good deal along the way.[17]

Generations of Americans have since lived their lives without ever having to deal with or even conceive of such wretched conditions, until now. Decades of demented liberal government have brought human feces back to our streets, thanks to lax laws and law enforcement related to the "homeless" in San Francisco. Readers of my books and listeners of my radio show, *The Savage Nation,* know this comes as no surprise.

Maybe San Francisco should have its own Statue of Liberty for the West Coast. Maybe it could be erected out by the Farallon Islands and could have its own inspiration poem: "Give us your addicted, your stupid, your worthless, your lazy, etc."

Time and again, I have warned of the dangers associated with chronic homelessness in our nation's cities. California's insane state and local liberal governments have allowed the homeless to overrun the streets. Liberals don't want people suffering from the effects of liberal policies to find out I predicted the catastrophes we're experiencing decades ago. They don't want the mental disorder cured. So, they steal my books.

Alternatively, it could be people who secretly agree with me who are doing the stealing. Imagine you are a liberal who has begun to suspect there is something very wrong with the liberal vision of society, with its Third World cityscapes, streets filled with used needles and human feces, unpunished crime, and fleeing businesses. Imagine you're an old-school, JFK liberal who sincerely believes one should ask what one can do for one's country, while you watch liberal psychopaths ask only what more they can do *to* your country. Imagine you wanted to know more about another vision for America, my vision, shared by tens of millions of patriots who don't want to live in the USSA or North Venezuela. Would you walk up to the judgmental, snooty liberal librarian and check out one of my books?

Unfortunately, it would be much safer for you to check both ends of the aisle to make sure no one is looking, slip my book under your coat, and spirit it out of the library. Better to commit petty larceny than to risk the librarian telling a mutual friend you were reading a banned book. Like their friends the radical Muslims, liberals treat apostates even worse than nonbelievers. Being shunned from polite liberal society might only be the beginning of the retribution. Your job and even your physical safety could be at risk. Just ask Brandon Straka, the gay former liberal who founded the #WalkAway movement, who was assaulted in an airport for wearing a Trump MAGA hat.[18]

VIOLENCE IS IN THE LEFT'S DNA

Of course, it has become commonplace for unhinged liberals to physically assault anyone wearing the iconic red ballcap with impunity and even approval from the liberal media. Breitbart has been keeping a running list of such media-approved assaults.[19] Some of the latest as of this writing include striking a fourteen-year-old boy wearing the red hat in the face and plowing a van into a Republican Party recruiting tent in which volunteers were registering people to vote. One poor schmuck was even attacked for *not* wearing the MAGA hat. He had a hat on that said, "Make Fifty Great Again." He was punched by a hysterical liberal woman who may have been holding keys or some other sharp object, judging by the wound the former NYPD officer sustained on his face.[20]

In February, police finally arrested the two violent left-ists who ran teenage twin boys on bicycles off the road in Indiana because the boys had pro-Trump flags attached to their bicycles.[21] The attack occurred the previous summer, but it took the police several months to track the perpetrators down through social media. The attackers, Kyren Gregory Perry-Jones, twenty-three, and Cailyn Marie Smith, eigh-teen, were driving a blue Chevy Malibu and reportedly ran the boys off the road and chased them through several yards, yelling, "Y'all scared, just like your president." Perry-Jones threatened to beat up the twins for calling 911 and then said that if questioned by police, he would claim the boys called him a racial slur.

Perry-Jones appears to be African American, based on the picture of him in the news story. Of course, I can't con-firm that from any media report about the incident because it is now established liberal media policy to never name the race of any minority perpetrator. Out of curiosity, I checked every news report I could find, including ABC News, the *Washington Post,* Yahoo News, and several local outlets. Not one of them—not even Fox News—mentions Perry-Jones's race.

I only mention this because it is particularly awkward for a news piece to report Perry-Jones's threat to tell police the boys used a racial slur and not report his race. Now, had the roles been reversed and a white driver forced two teenage African American boys off the road for displaying Obama flags, I have a feeling the racial background of the perpetra-tor would have received some attention. Don't you?

Not only would you know the perpetrator's race, but you'd likely still be hearing Jake Tapper and his fellow propagandists blathering about "white nationalist" violence and finding a way to blame it on the president. But this incident is reported with as little fanfare as possible, to be flushed down the memory hole as quickly as possible.

It's probably lucky for the victims the whole incident was caught on video. Otherwise, they might have been the next Covington High School case, further victimized by a libelous assault on their character for assaulting Perry-Jones!

These are only a few examples of the almost daily violence committed by the Left against traditional American individuals and institutions. How many times have I told you in the past that violence is an integral part of leftist ideology and has been since 1789? The guillotine, the mass murders in early-twentieth-century Russia and mid-twentieth-century China and Cambodia, the Weather Underground in 1970s America, and the 2016 riots at the sites of Trump rallies are all typical of leftist behavior. It is only when they are satiated with blind obedience to their doctrine that they are relatively peaceful. Any resistance to their policies, no matter how lawful and peaceable, is met with violence.

There is no conservative counterpart to Antifa or Black Lives Matter. When have you ever seen a conservative mob attack a Bernie Sanders supporter or vandalize an entire neighborhood? We just had the duly elected president of the United States impeached in a sham, partisan proceeding that allowed no witnesses for the defendant and no due process whatsoever, based on the president *doing his duty* to look into corruption involving the children of high-ranking Democrats. Where were the Trump supporters setting cars on fire, smashing shop windows, and assaulting liberals with clubs?

There weren't any, just as you didn't see any after either election of Barack Obama, the most divisive president in U.S. history. You didn't see it at any time during the eight long years he was president, doing his best to foment racial and class division. You didn't see it when he flooded the country with illegal immigrants, resorting to his "pen and phone" when Americans rose up and put Republicans in both houses of Congress to stop him. And you haven't seen it—yet—from conservatives in the face of left-wing assaults and mob violence perpetrated against their persons.

I warned during the Obama years that a civil war could come to America and only restraint on the part of conservatives has prevented it, despite the best efforts of the race baiters and envy peddlers on the left. So far, conservatives have stoically absorbed the violent attacks, choosing to appeal to authorities to lawfully prosecute the perpetrators. They haven't employed the Black Lives Matter strategy of burning down private businesses, many owned by blacks, to "protest" the injustice they've suffered.

But I live in fear that a day will come when conservatives refuse to turn the other cheek. That's the day Antifa learns they've brought a club to a gunfight and believe me, I don't relish the prospect. That's why my 2014 book was called *Stop the Coming Civil War*. If you haven't read that book, you should do so after you've finished this one. You can try to check it out of the library if it's still there.

This book will reach the shelves of stores and libraries (at least for a little while) just prior to the presidential election. I shudder to think of how much worse the rioting and mob violence will be this year compared to 2016. We had a chilling preview earlier this year when Republican candidate for Congress John Dennis, who is running against Speaker of the House Nancy Pelosi, was confronted by what he described as an "Antifa bully." Dennis shared videotape of the incident that showed this thug telling Dennis, "Imma catch you when all the cameras aren't around and I'm gonna f—k you up."[22]

Dennis attempted to engage the militant, asking why he hated Dennis so much. He was met with the usual, mindless accusation of being a racist, even though Dennis pointed out he had grown up in a public housing project. The thug repeatedly told Dennis to go home, that "we don't want you here in San Francisco," even though he's lived in San Francisco for over thirty years, perhaps longer than the militant has been alive. There is no reasoning with these people. All we can do is try to persuade those bamboozled by the left's claims of tolerance and inclusiveness that this is a fundamentally violent, authoritarian movement.

SILENCE IS NOT GOLDEN

Thomas Carlyle may have been the first to use the phrase "silence is golden" in English, translating it from German in his 1836 novel, *Sartor Resartus*. He said silence is "the element in which great things fashion themselves together." He went on to say that it is sometimes better for considerable men to say nothing at all than to "babble of what they were creating and projecting." He was talking about *self*-censoring, about refraining from going on and on when saying nothing at all might accomplish your goal better. Wouldn't it be nice if more people today heeded his wise advice?

Today we use the phrase "silence is golden" in a much wider sense. We live in a very noisy world and it's getting noisier all the time. I've seen a little bit of the history of this country in my time. I remember when you went to a doctor's office and there was not television playing in the waiting room. There was no such thing as "elevator music." Today, you can't even put gas in your car without being assaulted by blaring, electronic noise.

Why Americans seem to need to be constantly entertained during every second of their day is a subject for another book. God forbid a quiet, original thought made its way through their heads. Comrade Bernie and Occasional Cortex certainly wouldn't want that. None of the poison that spills out of their noisemakers would survive five minutes of quiet, thoughtful consideration.

Yes, today, a little silence is more golden than ever if you can find it. But that's only true when "silence" is used as a noun. Silence as a phenomenon is soothing, even spiritual. It connects one to the divine. But silence as a verb is quite another thing. "To silence" someone has been the modus operandi of every tyrant who ever lived. Silence as a verb always accompanies the jackboot and the gulag. That's why our founders strictly prohibited the government from silencing even its harshest critics with the very first amendment to the Constitution they had ratified.

But silence as a verb is the left's new policy and they don't even make a secret of it. They saw how my message of borders, language, and culture spread like wildfire over social media once it was adopted by a certain Republican presidential candidate in 2016. And yes, Donald Trump won by campaigning on my message. Members of the administration told me this just after he was elected. "We read your books and simplified them for a mass audience," said one high-level administration official. But no one who has been listening to my show, *The Savage Nation,* or was reading my books long before Donald Trump decided to run for office needs the administration to tell them that. It's obvious.

All things being equal, the table is set for a repeat of 2016. Given the senile hologram in the basement they've chosen as their nominee, the Democrats could lose even bigger this year than they did the last time, although I have cautioned conservatives not to get too overconfident. One reason is all things are not equal, especially the right to express one's opinion. The left has decided that since their nonsense cannot defeat common sense and reason, the latter must be driven from the public square. And they've come up with a rather clever way of doing so: teaming up with the lefties who run giant social media companies who have used monopoly privileges to become the new public square.

You must give these devils their due. By teaming up with private sector companies, they have created a strategy that they believe is impervious to attack from conservatives. Since Google, Twitter, and Facebook are private property, they try to pass off these monopolistic giants erasing conservative voices from the public square as an outcome of the free market. Superficially, that seems plausible. Unfortunately, "superficially" is about as deep as too many Americans go these days. Almost half don't even bother to vote and, believe me, only a tiny percentage of those people are refraining for some principled reason. Most just expect the free, prosperous nation we've had to be there for their enjoyment without any effort.

Well, it's going to take those of us willing to fight for this country to put in a much bigger effort to get our message out to sympathetic ears this time around. That's because Silicon Valley has perfected its program to stamp out conservative voices. It's really very simple. They simply label anyone to the right of Alexandria Occasional Cortex as a "white nationalist" or "alt right extremist" and then claim such people are violating their terms of service with "hate speech" or "aggressive behavior."

They were smart enough to start with a few genuine white nationalists or alt-right extremists to set the precedent. That's the way totalitarians always start shutting down speech. First, they find someone virtually everyone condemns. Who is going to complain if a social media platform bans members of the Ku Klux Klan? No one wants to hear from them anyway. But banning speech even from a Klan member or white nationalist, provided it is not truly threatening violence, is very dangerous ground because you've given up the principle of free speech.

Banning speech is very much in the same vein. Once you conceded that it is okay to ban speech almost everyone finds offensive, the door is open to banning speech not quite as offensive. Then, speech that isn't offensive at all. This is how authoritarians work. This is how the left is working on you right now.

This isn't some wild conspiracy theory I read about on the Internet. This has happened to yours truly. In addition to my website, www.MichaelSavage.com, I have a Twitter account (@ASavageNation) with just over two hundred thousand followers as of this writing. It's not the biggest following on Twitter by any stretch, but I wasn't eager to jump into what is largely a cesspool of stupidity. I joined and established an account because I had to do so to remain relevant as a political commentator. I have millions of listeners on my radio show, but Twitter has billions of accounts, including hundreds of millions of Americans.

Last year, the West sustained another mortal wound when Notre Dame in Paris burned. This iconic cathedral is more than just a church. It's a symbol of the glory of Western culture at its finest. And Notre Dame wasn't alone. The incident in April 2019 was just the latest in a series of undisputed attacks on Catholic churches across France, attacks that "included arson and desecration," according to approved liberal media outlet *Newsweek*.[23]

Not to be outdone, Black Lives Matter protestors have repeatedly vandalized St. John's Church in Washington, D.C., the "church of presidents." First, they tried to burn it down during the first round of "protests in late May and then defaced with graffiti in a second attack in late June."[24] This is a Marxist organization, so we shouldn't be surprised when even churches aren't spared their destruction.

The article claims officials don't know why the attacks are occurring, but it doesn't take a lot of curiosity to come up with a list of suspects. Buried in the article is an admission by the executive director of the Vienna-based Observatory of Intolerance and Discrimination Against Christians in Europe that France faced increasing violence against Christians, "especially by anarchist and feminist groups."

In other words, our violent friends on the left.

I can think of one other group that might contain some "persons of interest" in any investigation into anti-Christian violence and vandalism: the members of a certain "religion of peace" who have recently mass immigrated into Europe. But no, the official ministers of truth ruled out all the above almost immediately after Notre Dame began burning, pronouncing the incident an accident.

You probably guessed I wasn't ready to close the case so fast. I posted my own opinions on Twitter, including this fateful tweet:

why do I say "TERRORISTS SET NOTRE DAME ABLAZE"? in 2016 3 RADICAL ISLAMISTS WERE CAUGHT IN FRONT OF THE CATHEDRAL WITH GAS CANNISTERS IN THEIR CAR. ARRESTED TRIED AND SENTENCED JUST LAST WEEK

Well, apparently that bit of common sense was too much for the liberal Thought Police over at Twitter. Immediately, my many thousands of followers began no longer seeing my tweets, including this one. Yes, they were still there, but through behind-the-scenes manipulation of its algorithms, Twitter was able to steer the tweet away from even my own followers seeing it.

That, in layman's terms, is what is called "shadow banning." It isn't just Twitter that is engaged in this practice. Google and Facebook are doing something similar. Facebook's approach is more like Twitter's: muting posts they don't like so that even one's "friends" or "followers" on their platform don't see them. Google's approach may be even more sinister, because they disappear conservative content from even a simple web search.

Just try to find a conservative perspective on a controversial news story. Sometimes, you can. But when the Thought Police have decided they only want one perspective—their left-wing perspective—suddenly web searches on Google become fruitless. Sure, if you already know the name of the article, video, or other content it may come up. But a general search on a controversial topic will return only the liberal versions of the story.

Like it or not, Twitter, Facebook, and Google have become the new political media. As I've been saying for some time, the traditional media is dying, largely because Americans are wise to them being mostly propaganda for the left-globalist elite. People prefer to get their news direct, without it being filtered through Wolf Blitzer's addled liberal brain.

Now, in a vibrant free market where Twitter had dozens of competitors, I would never have opened an account and I wouldn't be writing this part of the book right now. I would simply join a fairer platform that gave me an equal chance to express my views. And I wouldn't want one that de-platformed liberals, either. I have many liberals call into my show to disagree with me. If they're honest and reasonable, I give them a fair hearing, even if I disagree in response. That's the way a free society works.

But there is no competitor for Twitter. There is not one option out there that would allow someone whose views Twitter wants to ban to reach anywhere near the number of people. The same goes for Facebook and Google. Democrats like to paint conservatives as wanting something beyond even laissez-faire free markets, that we would just let corporations run wild without any accountability. This is at best ignorance.

Let's not forget it was Republicans who wrote and passed the Sherman Anti-Trust Act. It was a Republican president who created the Environmental Protection Agency (EPA). And contrary to their constant slanders of Republicans as racists or even "white supremacists," 82 percent of Republicans voted for the Civil Rights Act of 1964, helping it pass despite only 61 percent of Democrats voting yes and many Democrat senators filibustering to stop it in the Senate.

I believe in free markets when they are truly free, with no special privileges and no barriers to entry. While these privileged multinational corporations enjoy the near monopoly they do, then the federal government must step in and protect the first and most basic right protected in the Bill of Rights. These tech giants are now in essence public utilities. Either regulate these companies just like all other news media and publishers are regulated or use antitrust laws to break them up.

NINE

THE PHONY MODERATE

WE'RE ALL SOCIALISTS NOW

When socialism came to America, it wasn't ushered in by that soup-stained, street corner communist, Bernie Sanders. It wasn't crazy-eyed Alexandria Occasional Cortex. No, socialism came to America silently, riding a serious but far from terrifying virus called SARS-CoV-2, which causes Covid-19, popularly known as "the coronavirus."

Socialism came in through the back door and suddenly the federal government was spending $2 trillion on handouts for everybody. Even this wasn't good enough for the witch, Nancy Pelosi, who slow-walked the bill through the House once it passed in the Senate. This was a bill that was proposed at $1 trillion and ballooned up to $2 trillion during the "compromise" period. For anyone who thinks compromise in government means nobody gets everything they want, they have it backward. Compromise in our government means every politician gets everything he or she wants, regardless of whether taxpayers want it.

As late as March 21, the proposed stimulus plan was only $1 trillion.[1] When it passed just four days later, it was $2 trillion. Why? Because as Barack Obama's chief of staff Rahm Emanuel once said, "never let a crisis go to waste." The Democrats certainly didn't. But neither did the Republicans. Pelosi got $50 million into the bill for the Kennedy Center. She asked for $300 million for refugee resettlement and the Republicans gave her $350 million. There is $150 million for the National Endowment for the Arts (NEA) and Humanities (NEH), along with $75 million for the Corporation for Public Broadcasting, aka DBS (Democrat Broadcasting System). There is more than $1 billion for Amtrak, which the government manages at a loss even during economic booms.[2]

Why did NPR get any money? This would have been a time to cut NPR off from public funds altogether if the Republicans really cared about fiscal sanity. It's one thing to bail out workers who are ordered by the government not to work, or businesses ordered by the government not to operate. I'm 1,000 percent for that. But why NPR, a fundamentally un-American, pro-world government institution? There is nothing more socialist than government-funded media. Think Pravda, think Chinese state-owned media. It's not any different just because it's done in America.

More particularly, everyone involved in public broadcasting hates Trump. Why didn't the Republicans cross out the entire line item providing funds for them? Because Madame Pelosi would have held the whole bill for ransom. Like I said before, compromise in government means everyone gets what they want except taxpayers. Madame Pelosi made sure the lying, communist broadcasting system got its turn at the trough.

All this graft and much more is in the bill voted into law 96–0 by the Republican-controlled Senate. Mitch McConnell got FDA approval for "innovative sunscreens," made by L'Oréal, which has operations in Kentucky. Even the casinos, excluded from disaster relief after Katrina, got in on the action. The bill allows them to access government-backed loans.[3]

Do you remember Patrick Leahy, the other senator from Vermont besides the soup-stained communist Bernie Sanders? "Leaky Leahy" got a provision into this monstrosity to guarantee that no state, no matter how small, would get less than $1.5 billion. How? Leahy used his leverage as a senator to see that Vermont got the same amount of relief money as California, even though Vermont has a population of just over half a million people. California has just under 40 million.

What happened to Vermont? It used to be one of the greatest states in the union. Now it elects two good-for-nothing mooks to the Senate every year. Early in the American Revolution, it was the Green Mountain Boys of Vermont who captured Fort Ticonderoga, which would later supply the cannons Washington used to kick the British out of Boston. Today, it seems like Vermonters would just as soon hand the fort over to Raul Castro or Nicolas Maduro, based on the way they vote.

Regardless, this is how government works. It's job security for the senators, job security for the congresspeople, and the American people get screwed. Never forget what I taught you a number of years ago: one of the most terrifying words in the government dictionary is "bipartisan." When both parties agree on something, you can be pretty sure the average American is getting the shaft.

Collateral damage is to be expected during any crisis. When there is a war, a flood, an earthquake, or a hurricane, there is collateral damage, including a lot of graft mixed in with genuine relief. But in this case, the collateral damage has been our liberty and our fiscal sanity. The collateral damage from this coronavirus may be worse than the virus itself.

The worst part about it is it's not going to work. Yes, the government depleting what's left of our accumulated wealth in one, last-gasp relief package may keep the lights on for another week or another month. But it can't undo the damage done by most of America being ordered to stop producing goods and services for an extended period of time. No handout can fix that.

This country is never going to be the same. There is no going back to normal. The past is dead. As of March 2020, we're all socialists and this is a socialist nation. All the small businesses that we've come to rely on and who employ most Americans are going to be gone. They were living week to week before this happened. They had no reserves. They were already being taxed out of business in San Francisco before this outbreak: a flower tax, a tablecloth tax, an AIDS tax, a health tax, high minimum wages. Eventually, this came along and finished them off.

I suppose the cities of San Francisco and New York could open public restaurants. New York could have the Cuomo Restaurant chain. Out here in California we could have the Newsom Cafeteria chain. Wouldn't that be wonderful? What could be better than the people who run the Department of Motor Vehicles running your restaurants? I can't wait for the Soviet-style service.

I should take a moment to point out that what was going on during these lockdowns wasn't socialism or capitalism. It was insanity. Under socialism, the government controls the means of production, decides how much of everything to make, and generally operates in the dark without market prices to guide them or market discipline to control them. That's why social-ist countries are so poor. But people are still working. They are still producing *something*, even if they are being directed to produce too much, too little, or the wrong things.

We just had state governors order a large portion of the population to stop producing anything at all. No government relief program can relieve that. The government can't redis-tribute zero. That some were calling for this to go on for sev-eral months amounts to a death cult, not socialism. How long do these people believe any population can produce nothing at all and survive?

THE ELECTORAL PENDULUM SWINGS SOCIALIST

Even the socialists who pervade our political class wouldn't let this go on forever. They need people producing some wealth or there would be nothing to rob. The end result, though, of the insane reaction to the virus is the permanent destruction of a large chunk of small businesses, their market share taken over by big corporations mostly run by left-wing ideologues. That sends another large portion of the population onto the permanent welfare rolls. Once there, we know which party gets their votes: the party promising more welfare.

Do you see what is happening? Donald Trump won the last election by a landslide in terms of electoral votes. But he won several critical states by razor-thin margins. All it takes is 1 percent or 2 percent in those states to change to Democrat and the electoral landslide switches to the other side. Add in some red states where once-independent, prosperous populations are now dependent upon the government to survive and you can see where this is going. All of America could become one-party California in the blink of an eye.

Let me remind you of a little "ancient" history. Yes, Donald Trump's win in 2016 was historic. It was a shot heard 'round the world, as I wrote in *Trump's War* just after his election. But don't forget how he did it. He got votes from many people in Rust Belt states who voted for Obama in 2012. Why? According to a poll cited by the *Washington Post,* a "shockingly large percentage of these Obama-Trump voters said Democrats' economic policies will favor the wealthy—twice the percentage that said the same about Trump."[4] They saw Trump in 2016 as someone more interested in fighting for their economic interests than was Hillary Clinton.

Even Bernie Sanders recognized this at the time. He went so far as to say the Democrats and liberal media were wrong to portray Trump voters as racists, sexists, and homophobes. He said the Democrat Party lost the election because they had become the party of the wealthy elite and working-class voters stayed home or voted Trump.[5] For once, the street corner communist was right about something.

Trump convinced disaffected working people in "flyover states" he could make capitalism work for them, based on his platform of America First economic nationalism. Even then there was speculation Sanders might have won those voters for the Democrats that Hillary couldn't and beaten Trump in the general election.[6]

I doubt that's true. Two thousand sixteen was Donald Trump's moment. It was America's moment to declare itself American again. But it can't be dismissed out of hand. What if these voters are so beaten up by the system they'd just as soon vote for a communist as a capitalist, as long as they think they're getting something different?

Regardless, that was then and this is now. We started this election year with the strongest economy we've had in decades, with unemployment at record lows and the stock market making record highs. Liberal governors ended all that in the space of one week by literally ordering the economy to collapse. In the blink of an eye, they took away the biggest advantage any incumbent president has. And they did it without so much as a whimper from the public.

Whether it was intentional or not, it couldn't have happened at a better time for the Democrats. Let me tell you two things about voters. They vote based upon their economic interests and they have chronic amnesia. By November, it isn't going to matter that the coronavirus wasn't Donald Trump's fault or even that they believe he handled it well. If they are hurting economically, they're going to vote against the incumbent unless there is a compelling reason to vote for him.

That will be especially true for voters who until 2016 normally voted Democrat. It took an extreme amount of dissatisfaction, extreme hubris by the Democrat Party, and one of the most unlikable candidates in history for them to pull the lever for Trump. This time around, they may be in even worse economic shape than they were in 2016, albeit because of artificially imposed conditions. Trump will have to completely heal the economy by then or convince them none of this was his fault and his plan is still the best for them. That both those things are true will make little difference. The booming economy we had in January was the much stronger hand.

The other warning sign is traditionally red states turning blue. Donald Trump won Arizona by a healthy 4 percent margin in 2016, and that was with an additional 4 percent going to Libertarian Party candidate Gary Johnson. But look at what has happened since then. Democrat Kyrsten Sinema defeated Republican Martha McSally in the 2018 Senate race. McSally is trailing Democrat Mark Kelly for the other Arizona Senate seat by more than seven points as of this writing.[7] That doesn't bode well for a Republican to win the state in the presidential election later this year.

Colorado and much of the mountain West is also turning blue. In Colorado's case, it isn't just because the whole population is stoned, although that could be as good a reason as any. No, the reason you're seeing the rugged West, Texas, and several other states turn from red to purple or purple to blue is immigration. I'm not talking about illegal immigration across our national borders, which is a separate electoral problem. I'm talking about liberal immigration across our state borders.

Ironically, Democrats are so bad at running their own states that they may never lose another presidential election again. Populations are flooding out of high-tax, highly regulated states like California and New York and into once-staunchly Republican states like Arizona. They run from the liberal policies that made their states hellholes, but they bring their liberal mental disorder with them.

As just one example, Ted Cruz only narrowly defeated Irish fake Latino Beto O'Rourke by a narrow margin in 2018.

CNN exit polls showed he got a lot of help from recent movers, with 60 percent of those who moved to Texas in the past ten years voting for O'Rourke.[8] Conservatives have all kinds of excuses for this, but it's not the only example. The five fastest-growing metropolitan areas in the United States right now are Dallas, Phoenix, Houston, Atlanta, and Orlando, Florida, all in states won by Trump in 2016.[9]

Let me tell you something: they're mostly importing liberals fleeing blue states like California, New York, New Jersey, and Illinois. According to the U.S. Census Bureau, ten states lost population in 2019. While only six of ten were blue states, 80 percent of the population losses came from those six states.[10]

Now look at the ten states that had the most population growth, according to the Census Bureau. They were Texas, Florida, Arizona, North Carolina, Georgia, Washington, Colorado, South Carolina, Tennessee, and Nevada. Seven out of ten of those went for Trump in 2016 and, more importantly, over 83 percent of the population growth occurred in states Trump won. This is overall population growth, so it is not exclusively people coming from other states. Natural increase—the difference between births and deaths—is still the number one contributor to population increase.[11] But virtually all increase from immigration, whether from out of state or abroad, represents almost exclusively new Democrat voters.

Maybe that's all too statistically detailed for you. I know most people aren't as trained to examine evidence as I am. So, let me sum it up for you. Economic conditions caused by liberal governors, combined with both international and intranational migration patterns and other demographics, could combine for the perfect storm in November. You could have the worst depression since at least the 1930s peaking while newly arrived liberals turn red states blue to produce a Democrat landslide just ten months after the economy was booming and the world was at relative peace under Trump.

MARXISTS IN MODERATE CLOTHING

A slim Democrat victory would be bad enough. Depending upon what happened in Congress, we may have to endure a return to the Obama years. God forbid it was like his first two years, when the Democrats had the House, Senate, and White House. But we have to consider what would happen if the Democrats won a sizeable victory or a landslide. I'm sure you can guess what the media would be saying before the votes were even done being counted. "President Biden (or Cuomo?) has a clear mandate for his agenda."

It won't really matter at that point what the exit polls say. It might not even matter if the Democrat victory was by that large a margin. With the useless excuse we have for an independent media, they may call 50 percent to 49 percent a mandate. And tens of millions of liberal voters will believe them.

If you're thinking to yourself it might not be that bad because Dementia Joe beat Comrade Bernie by so much in the primaries, think again. We've all been sold the idea that the moderate beat the revolutionary, that the regulated capitalism candidate beat the socialist. Well, I hate to rain on that parade, but guess again. Biden is not that far from Sanders when you compare their policies side by side.

Let's start with arguably the most insane proposal ever to emerge from the dark recesses of the far left, the Green

New Deal. This is the totalitarian mad dream proposed by that Stalinist in a Skirt, Alexandria Occasional Cortex. The one where every building in America—including private homes—gets rebuilt to be more energy efficient. It's the plan to impoverish the entire country in order to get to "net zero greenhouse gas emissions" within ten years. In case you don't remember, they're only shooting for net zero instead of absolute zero because they don't think they can do anything about "bovine flatulence."

Thank goodness for cow farts or it might be even worse.

Now, it's not surprising this unhinged plot seems just fine to Occasional Cortex's fellow communist Bernie Sanders. He acknowledges he would like to enact all the worst parts of it, including rebuilding every private home in America. Of course, that suggestion received so much ridicule that he hides it this way on his website:

> Save American families money with investments in weatherization, public transportation, modern infrastructure and high-speed broadband.[12]

This is his roundabout way of saying what the infamous Green New Deal FAQ Fact Sheet said before it was hurriedly taken down by the Democrats amid a tornado of criticism: "Upgrade or replace every building in US for state-of-the-art energy efficiency."[13] Never mind the trillions this would cost. Do you really want this insane communist in charge of redesigning your home?

That grim prospect is relatively mild compared to the reality of achieving net zero emissions by 2030. That would require banning fossil fuels, including relatively clean-burning natural gas, which has helped the United States lead the world in greenhouse gas emissions per capita.[14] But that it's counterproductive is the least of its problems. This ban would literally plunge all but the richest of the rich into abject poverty.

The respected, center-right *InsideSources* estimates that the Green New Deal would cost typical households in Florida, New Hampshire, New Mexico, and Pennsylvania more than $70,000 the first year it is implemented, $45,000 the second year, and $37,000 every year after that.[15] In other states your costs could vary. Maybe in yours you could get away with just $60,000 the first year and $30,000 after that. I'm sure most Americans have that lying around, burning a hole in their pockets.

This one plank of the Green Manifesto would also cost 5.9 million jobs and reduce gross domestic product (GDP) by $11.8 trillion. That's after the new so-called green jobs are factored in.[16] And as if the economic damage wasn't bad enough, this psychotic proposal also bans 99 percent of automobiles, all air travel, and meat.[17] That's right, to get those cow farts under control, Der Kommissar Cortex is no longer going to allow you to eat meat.

Listeners to my show, *The Savage Nation*, know that I've recently made the decision to no longer eat anything with eyes. That was a personal decision I made for health and compassion reasons. That decision was right for me. I don't claim to have the wisdom nor the right to make that decision for you. You want to eat meat? Go ahead. Eat all you want. We'd all appreciate it if you avoid bats, though.

That decision won't be up to you in the new, socialist utopia. But don't worry. After you lose your home because you can't pay the light bills, Comrade Cortex will have a government house and job for you. She'll even provide you with healthy food and your children with free college—if they can find a seat in the classroom full of illegal immigrants.[18]

There is much more to this communist monstrosity, but I don't want to rehash it all again after doing so when it was first proposed. Suffice it to say the Green New Deal is the superficial excuse for a complete, socialist takeover of the American economy. It will do in the first year what sometimes takes decades in socialist countries: reduce most of the population to abject poverty.

It's a good thing the Democrats aren't going to nominate Bernie Sanders, right? Well, let me share with you a direct quote from "moderate" Joe Biden's website:

> Biden believes the Green New Deal is a crucial framework for meeting the climate challenges we face. It powerfully captures two basic truths, which are at the core of his plan: (1) the United States urgently needs to embrace greater ambition on an epic scale to meet the scope of this challenge, and (2) our environment and our economy are completely and totally connected.[19]

Oh, did that surprise you? You didn't know Moderate Joe also supported the insane Green New Deal. All it takes is a couple of clicks on his campaign website to see how similar he is to the soup-stained communist. The same page I quoted above also talks about a "Clear Energy Revolution," and rebuilding "roads, bridges, buildings, the electric grid, and our water infrastructure."

It says he will sign executive orders to see the nation gets to net zero emissions by 2050, so the deadline is twenty years later than Occasional Cortex's, but the principle is the same. It will still reduce most of America to poverty, just not quite as quickly. Biden's website also says his plan "establishes an enforcement mechanism to achieve the 2050 goal, including a target no later than the end of his first term in 2025 to ensure we get to the finish line."

So, he's going to be terrorizing the economy by the end of his first term in order to pursue the mad dream of powering this entire nation with wind and solar power.

Is all this a surprise to you? Let me tell you something. The narrative that the moderate defeated the socialist is one of the greatest bait-and-switch schemes ever perpetrated on the American public. The Green New Deal is just the beginning.

Most people are aware Sanders has promised to cancel all existing student loan debt and "guarantee tuition and debt-free public colleges, universities, HBCUs, Minority Serving Institutions and trade-schools to all."[20] The cost is in the trillions for a government already more than $23 trillion in debt before the massive Covid-19 handouts. Again, people probably assume "Moderate" Joe's policy is significantly different. Well, read for yourself what his website says about this:

> Joe will provide two years of community college or other high-quality training program without debt for any hard-working individual looking to learn and improve their skills. He will also make four-year

public colleges and universities tuition-free for all students whose family incomes are below $125,000.[21]

So, Biden will only give free college to students whose family incomes are below $125,000. That's certainly more "moderate" than Comrade Bernie giving it away to everyone, right? Wrong. Just put your thinking cap on for a moment. Just how many students that Bernie would give a free ride would Biden's policy exclude? Not that many.

The "Don't Quit Your Day Job" website provides a household income calculator that says households earning $125,000 per year are at the 78th percentile.[22] That is roughly consistent with the U.S. Census figure that puts households earning over $130,000 in the highest quintile (highest 20 percent).[23] So, it's safe to assume about 78 percent of U.S. households earn less than $125,000 per year.

So, the democratic socialist is going to give tuition-free college to everyone and the supposed moderate is going to give it to almost 80 percent of everyone.

I could do this for every one of Sanders's and Biden's policies, but I'll compare just one more. Everyone knows Bernie Sanders wants to sign "Medicare for All" into law. He'd instantly put every private health insurance company out of business and make government employees of every doctor, nurse, and medical technician in America. Yes, I know the practices would still be privately owned, but when the government is the sole source of revenue, with all others legally prohibited, you're a government employee in all but name.

You could say the government would own the means of production for health insurance. So, it's not surprising the

soup-stained Marxist likes the idea. Well, guess what. Dementia Joe likes it, too. He just doesn't want to get rid of private
insurance companies on day one, like Sanders does. Instead,
he wants to offer the communist plan as a "public option,"
whereby those who want to keep their private health insurance can do so.[24]

This sounds great, doesn't it? You only have to go on the
government plan if you want to. That gives everyone who has
other options a choice, right?

This might be the greatest scam of all and I can hear Conservative Inc. falling for it hook, line, and sinker. "A government plan will never compete with our wonderful free market
health care insurance plans! Never!" Then follows the cigar
smoke belly laugh.

First, I don't need to tell you what we have now isn't a free
market. It wasn't even a free market before Obamacare. But
the key here is that this won't be competition on a level playing field. Do you really believe that if costs go up beyond what
the government sets as its initial premium, the premiums will
go up as well? It's a rigged game, a stacked deck. The private
health insurers either manage risk well or go out of business.
The government plan won't face that market discipline. If it
loses money, the government will simply force those not in the
plan to cover the losses.

How do I know this? Because that's the way Medicare
works. In 2018, only 56 percent of Medicare's costs were paid
by payroll taxes, premiums, and other receipts.[25] That means
that just barely half of the program's costs were covered by
the money collected for the program. The rest was paid for
out of the government's general fund.

Do you think that is how Medicare was originally sold? Of course not. The payroll tax is supposed to cover the entire program. That's what taxpayers were told when it was implemented. But as the costs skyrocketed, politicians didn't have the courage to level with the public about how much more they would have to pay for this "popular" government-run health plan. So, they simply allowed the financing to change so that the progressive income tax picks up the difference.

That works well if you're a politician. Seventy percent of the income taxes collected are paid by the top 10 percent of income earners. The bottom 50 percent pay almost no income taxes. You can see where it would improve a politician's odds to transfer the costs of the goodies he promised to as small a portion of the voting public as possible. The only incentive he'd have to level with the public and ask them to pay for the benefits was his personal integrity.

Fat chance, that.

There is no reason a "public option" for health insurance wouldn't work the same way. Yes, there would be a propaganda campaign showing how it would pay for itself out of the premiums collected from those who opted in. Those premiums would be lower, according to the Marxists in Moderate Clothing, because they would be eliminating the extra costs of marketing and profit. So why don't we have the government run everything, eliminating marketing and profit from the cost of all goods and services?

Oh yeah, that's been tried. It was called the Soviet Union.

What will really happen once a public option is available to the public is the costs will quickly begin outpacing the revenues collected in premiums. The difference will be covered by taxpayers not enrolled in the program. Eventually, the private health insurance companies, who have to cover 100 percent of their costs through premiums, will be unable to compete with the public option. Taxpayers paying half the cost of the public option on top of their own health insurance premiums will start asking themselves why they are paying for health insurance twice and opt into the government plan. Biden's public option will eliminate private health insurance just as surely as Bernie's, just not as quickly or as honestly.

The hard truth is there is no moderate candidate in the Democrat Party. Not Joe Biden and not Andrew Cuomo if he is substituted for Biden in a brokered convention, as is being whispered in certain circles now, even though Cuomo himself denies it.[26] The hard left has taken control of the Democrat Party and apparently it is impossible to win without adopting most of their agenda, even if the so-called moderate tries to call it something else.

Donald Trump has said, "America will never be a socialist country." Well, I have news for you. Unless we can get him reelected, it will, no matter which Democrat takes the oath in 2021.

TEN

FROM LAW AND ORDER TO RAW DISORDER:

HOW THE LEFT STOLE ELECTIONS AND OUR NATION'S HERITAGE

THE PREEMPTIVE COUP

As America limps toward the November elections, cowed into submission by lunatic, cryptofascist governors and terrorized by armies of street thugs given free rein to loot and burn public buildings and privately held businesses, with one far-left group even seizing part of the city of Seattle, it's understandable if some people wonder how we got here. I don't. I know how we got here because I've watched and reported on the cryptofascist left for more than twenty-five years. Nothing they're doing is new. It's the same "let it burn, baby" strategy they've been employing since the 1960s.

Yes, they've ramped up the intensity during this election year, but we've watched an ongoing coup attempt against President Trump since before he even took the oath of office.

The party that calls itself "Democratic" is the least democratic organization on the face of the earth. First, they tried stealing the election with millions of phony votes from illegal immigrants and dead people. When that failed, they tried to cash in on their "insurance policy," the debunked conspiracy theory that the president and his campaign colluded with the Russian government to influence American voters through social media and other means.

While any collusion with Russia by President Trump or his campaign was debunked by the Establishment's own investigation, the ironic part of the allegation is that nobody denies the information provided to American voters was untrue. It consisted of authentic emails written and received by Hillary Clinton herself, along with members of that criminal cabal known as the Democratic National Committee. So, the president was accused of colluding with Russia to provide accurate information about a presidential candidate to the American public. "Never mind that," says the bought-and-sold national media. "Donald Trump is an illegitimate president." And millions of useful idiots nod their heads in agreement.

It's hard to believe Robert Mueller concluded his report without recommending any further indictments just last year. So much has happened since then that it seems like a distant memory. But don't be deceived. Virtually everything that has happened since Mueller held his final press conference in May 2019 has been the left at work seeking to nullify two elections: the one in 2016 that put Donald Trump in the White House and the one in 2020 that will put him there again, if the Democrats can't manufacture a win for their dementia-addled shadow candidate.

Coups are as old as government itself, but I can't think of a single instance where the subversives began trying to overthrow a legitimate executive before he even won an election. The southern states in America seceded before Lincoln was inaugurated, but at least they waited until he was elected. The Democrats' coup against Trump started before he was even *nominated,* with the FBI's corrupt "investigation" into the Trump administration's supposed collusion with Russia to influence the 2016 election.

None of the criminals in that phase of the plot have been brought to justice yet, but the FISA Court has acknowledged the Justice Department's official admission that at least two of the four warrants to surveil Trump campaign staffer Carter Page were invalid.[1] Not only does this confirm the FBI's wrongdoing, but it could potentially nullify some or all of the convictions resulting from Mueller's two-year witch hunt.[2]

Eventually, it will be publicly acknowledged that the whole investigation, from the first surveillance of Trump campaign personnel to Mueller's doddering testimony to Congress, was an illegal covert operation against the electoral process itself.

This was a coup against not only candidate and then President Trump, but against our Constitution and republican form of government. It was those same elites who had dismissed the Eddies and the Ediths for so long, had wagged their self-important fingers at them for "clinging to their guns and religion," all the while selling them out to multinational corporations who sent their jobs to China and Mexico. We nominated Trump and they said, "Oh, you think you're going to change something by electing an outsider? Think again. We're taking him down."

THE IMPEACHMENT HOAX

After wasting over two years and $32 million in taxpayer funds, the first attempt to overthrow the election failed. In most countries, members of a failed coup are prosecuted. But in progressive America, some get jobs on television at left-wing propaganda outlets like NBC and CNN.[3] The rest are simply congratulated for their crimes and sent off to try again.

And try again they did, without even taking much time off. Almost the minute Russiagate crashed and burned, as we always knew it would, the Democrats came up with a new conspiracy theory, this time centered on an innocuous phone call with the president of Ukraine. Mueller submitted his report to Attorney General Bill Barr in March 2019;[4] but he didn't officially close the investigation until May 22 of that year.[5] That left just fifty-seven days, less than two months, before the July 25, 2019, phone call from Trump to Ukrainian president Volodymyr Zelensky,[6] over which the Democrats impeached a president.

This, by the way, was not the Establishment's second major attempt to overthrow the elected government. It was at least the third. Just a few months after Trump's inauguration, members of his own administration were plotting to remove him under Article XXV.[7] Remember that? This was supposedly in response to the president being "unstable" for having fired that criminal gang leader, James Comey. Now, even Comey admits his FBI was incompetent, or in his words, "overconfident," in seeking FISA warrants to spy on the Trump campaign, although he wants you to believe there was no ill intent.[8] If there is any justice in this world, this man's day in court is coming, followed by a couple of decades in an orange jumpsuit.

It might be easy for an honest person who just arrived in this country to take this impeachment conflict seriously if he didn't know the history of this presidency. Outside of Fox News, the media reported this hoax as if it were an open-and-shut case against Trump. Not only that, they consistently called the allegations against Hunter Biden's corruption "a debunked conspiracy theory."

Here's a news flash for anyone whose memory only extends three weeks into the recent past: *Russia collusion* is a debunked conspiracy theory. That one was debunked by the conspiracy theorists themselves when they couldn't find a shred of evidence Donald Trump or his campaign colluded with the Russians to influence the 2016 election. But you won't ever hear the lying media use that term for the Russia hoax. Of course not. They'd be telling the truth.

The corruption of the Bidens, on the other hand, is precisely the opposite. Don't forget that many conspiracy theories turn out to be true. Our prisons are full of convicts who were convicted of conspiracy. But most of them don't hold a candle to what Clan Biden has pulled off at the expense of the American taxpayer.

I had Peter Schweizer on my show, *The Savage Nation,* back in January. He's the author of *Clinton Cash*, the blockbuster exposé on Bill and Hillary's supposed charitable foundation that laundered bribes from foreigners from all over the world. Well, Schweizer came out with a new book called *Profiles in Corruption: Abuse of Power by America's Progressive Elite.* If you ever had any doubt President Trump was completely justified in seeking an investigation of Hunter Biden, then I suggest you read that book the minute you finish reading this one.

Schweizer's book goes beyond the corruption of the Biden family. It talks about Elizabeth Warren's son-in-law's secret deal with the Iranian Revolutionary Guard. Fake capitalist, fake socialist, fake Native American Fauxahontas herself bagged millions from corporations by leveraging her position as a government consultant. It even covers how street corner communist Bernie Sanders's campaign secretly flowed tens of millions of dollars to a company linked to his wife.

But the Biden family rivals the Clintons when it comes to lining their pockets at their country's expense. Schweizer says no fewer than five Biden family members have their snouts in the trough, including two of Creepy Joe's brothers, his sister, his daughter, and, of course, his son, Hunter.

Schweizer has devoted his career to exposing corruption in government—by both Democrats and Republicans, by the way—and the most members he can recall in a single family is three, outside the Biden gang. The game plan is simple. Find a corrupt country that wants something from the United States, get in bed with their oligarchs, and sell them what they want. They've done it all over the world. Hunter Biden did it in Ukraine, among other places.

Just look at the timeline of Biden's involvement in Ukraine. Somehow, Ukrainian gas company Burisma survived for twelve years without the help of Hunter Biden or his consulting firm, which was co-owned by John Kerry's stepson. Then, less than two months after democratically elected Ukrainian president Viktor Yanukovych was ousted from power in February 2014, Hunter Biden is suddenly a board member of the company.

Let's not forget that the coup that deposed Yanukovych had the Obama administration's fingerprints all over it.[9] Obama and the European Union wanted Yanukovych out because he was too friendly with Russia. So, Obama's State Department ran its patented regime-change-by-protest program that worked so well in the Middle East. Of course, the Obama administration denied all this, but no one in their right mind believes them. Assistant Secretary of State Victoria Nuland was recorded openly discussing plans for a new government in Ukraine with the U.S. ambassador to Ukraine, Geoffrey Pyatt.[10]

So, Obama overthrows the Ukrainian government and installs a U.S. puppet in Kiev in February 2014. Hunter Biden joins the board of Burisma in April 2014. Burisma and its founder, Mykola Zlochevsky, are the subjects of at least thirteen corruption investigations, including embezzling state funds, tax violations, money laundering, and licenses given to Burisma during the period where Zlochevsky was a minister.[11]

THE KANGAROO COURT

As corrupt as the Bidens may be, they don't hold a candle to Power Mad Pelosi and Shifty Adam Schiff. That they could have the temerity to not only excuse the Bidens' corruption but bring impeachment charges against the president for trying to investigate it is incredible. In the wake of the Corona Catastrophe and violent revolution that has taken place since, you may be tempted to think this is all water under the bridge.

It isn't. If the president wins the election this November, these traitors are going to be back trying to nullify that election, too. So, let's look at the facts of the whole impeachment charade:

A "whistleblower" filed a charge against the president saying the president said things in a phone call with Ukraine the whistleblower felt compromised national security. The media says it's a quid pro quo. Trump supposedly promised to hold back funds for weapons if Joe Biden's son wasn't investigated. They said the president mentioned it eight times.

Trump released a transcript of the call.[12] It doesn't even hint at a quid pro quo. Biden is mentioned once, not eight times, for completely legitimate reasons. President Trump wanted the Ukrainian president to investigate the circumstances surrounding the dismissal of a prosecutor looking into Hunter Biden's corruption, which Joe Biden himself bragged about accomplishing by doing the very thing President Trump was now accused of—withholding U.S. aid to Ukraine![13]

The whistleblower complaint was eventually released and did not match up with the transcript of the phone call at all. It turned out the so-called whistleblower never even heard the call. His complaint was based purely on secondhand information or worse.[14] Now, it is routine procedure for other members of the administration to listen in on a call such as this one and that is exactly what happened on July 25, 2019. Several members of the Trump administration, including Secretary of State Mike Pompeo, were listening in and had no concerns about the president's conversation with Zelensky.

Yet an impeachment proceeding was launched based on a complaint from someone who didn't even hear the call.

Eventually, Director of National Intelligence (DNI) Joseph Maguire appeared before Congress. That's when Adam Schiff made his now-infamous opening statement, completely misrepresenting what was in the transcript. There is no pushback for half an hour, and only then did Schiff say it was 'parody.'[15] So, Schiff lies into the congressional record over and over and then brushes off his deliberate attempt to mislead the House members and the American people as parody.

Not satisfied with that, he then goes on to attempt to browbeat Maguire into saying the whistleblower complaint has merit, but Maguire refuses to take the bait. Why would he? If the complaint had merit, Schiff wouldn't have felt the need to misrepresent the transcript in an official record.

Eventually, Pelosi called for an impeachment inquiry. But she did not bring that to the floor of the House to vote on because she didn't want to expose her moderate members.[16] So, it was never really so much an impeachment inquiry as a charade.

Once the transcript of the call was released, any honest person, even a liberal being honest with himself, would have dismissed the entire case against the president. But the cynical Democrats, half conniving and half crazed with hatred for the president, insisted on going all the way to an impeachment vote, knowing full well there wasn't a prayer of a conviction in the Senate. And the people Pelosi chose to lead this naked political attack couldn't represent its dishonesty better.

THE NIGHT SCHOOL NEBBISH

The day before the impeachment hearings began, House impeachment manager Jerry Nadler told his fellow Democrats he was not going to take any sh** during the impeachment hearings.[17] A real tough guy, right? Let me tell you who Jerry Nadler really is. He's nothing but a night school nebbish, trying to act tough and undo an election on false pretenses wrapped in lies and rigged testimony from Adam Schiff. He always looks like he just came out from behind a deli counter, where he was caught with his finger on the scale.

Nadler got his BA in government from Columbia, then worked as a legal assistant, and in 1972 got into politics as a legislative assistant for the New York State Assembly, but that wasn't good enough for him so he became a shift manager at New York's Off Track Betting. And where did Nadler get his law degree? At night school. At Fordham University School of Law.

Then he jumped into politics in 1977; he kept running for different positions and kept getting beat by possibly the worst mayor in New York City history until now, David Dinkins. It makes one wonder how he ever got into Congress. Here's how: a popular congressman running for reelection, Ted Weiss, died a day before the Democratic primary in New York, and they inserted Nadler in his place. He won by default.

He was a staunch defender of Bill Clinton during his impeachment in 1998, using many of the arguments to defend Clinton that he then used to try to discredit President Trump. During the Bush administration he made attempts to impeach

George W. Bush, but eventually gave up in 2007, saying that doing so would be pointless and would distract from the presidential election.[18]

The point is here is a man with no accomplishments to speak of, other than losing one hundred pounds. A small man in stature and accomplishments. A man with pants worn up to his chest, looking like a disheveled public defender who has lost too many of his cases. And now he wants to take down Donald Trump. But this feud is not just about a presidency. This is personal for the little nebbish, too.

In 1984, then-private businessman Donald Trump had big plans for a seventy-six-acre parcel of land along the Hudson River on Manhattan's Upper West Side. Trump envisioned 7,600 high-rise apartments, a shopping mall that would have been the largest on the east coast at the time, and a new studio complex for NBC. The crown jewel of this endeavor would have been a 152-story condominium. It would have been the tallest building in the world at the time and Trump planned on living in its penthouse.

It was an ambitious vision, like everything Donald Trump plans, and would have been a tremendous boon to New York City. But it was not to be. According to the *New York Post*:

> But while the real estate scion was poised to begin construction on the biggest residential development in New York City history, he faced rabid opposition from community groups led by an earnest, bespectacled 37-year-old lawmaker. In fact, Brooklyn-born Jerrold Nadler would prove Trump's fiercest enemy

for the next decade while he represented the Upper West Side as a state Assemblyman and later as its Congressman.[19]

According to *Slate,* "A crucial part of Trump's plan involved relocating a stretch of the West Side Highway, which would otherwise obstruct views of the Hudson River. The move, estimated to cost more than $300 million, would require federal funding. From his new perch in Washington, Nadler did all he could to block the subsidy."[20]

You'll never guess who else the Night School Nebbish appealed to for help in blocking Trump's project. This was during the Clinton years and President Clinton's secretary of housing and urban development was none other than Andrew Cuomo, now cryptofascist governor of New York. Nadler lobbied Cuomo to reject Trump's request for federal mortgage insurance because the condo would have no low-income units.[21] You aren't allowed to erect a beautiful building in a liberal city without distributing perks to Democrat voters.

Fast-forward a few decades and the night school nebbish, Jerry Nadler, who rose to power through luck and chance, eventually got appointed to head up the impeachment effort against a man he personally hates and has a grudge against. So much for impartial justice.

President Trump is someone who has created more jobs, wealth, resources, and goods than Jerry Nadler, the otherwise deli clerk. Nadler has not done anything of note to make the country better or to benefit any American in the country. And he was allowed to sit in judgment of your vote. He didn't like who you voted for, and he tried to undo it.

A REAL SCHIFF SHOW

Then there is Adam Schiff. What he perpetrated during the impeachment proceedings was an embarrassment to all the institutions we hold sacred. This noted liar led the inquiry into impeaching the president of the United States and was allowed to make all the rules.

He called two witnesses, Bill Taylor and George Kent, who, like the "whistleblower," were not even on the call to the president of Ukraine. In fact, neither of these men ever actually met the president, something even a CNN analyst admitted was "a problem."[22] So, why were they called? How was their testimony at all relevant to the case against the president?

It wasn't. This wasn't about truth, fairness, or due process. It was a political assassination attempt and Schiff hoped Taylor and Kent would say something damaging. Not legally damaging, mind you, but politically damaging.

Schiff did not have Congress do its due diligence to ask questions. Instead, he had Norman Eisen, a legal analyst for MSNBC and NBC, a platform that he uses to continuously criticize the president. This lawyer was a proponent of the Russia hoax and the Steele dossier.[23] Along with Eisen was Barry Berke, another vocal critic of the president long before the July 25, 2019, phone call.

The Republicans also asked their questions through an attorney, instead of directly. It is not the norm to cede the power of the people to a paid shill to conduct one of the most important responsibilities of Congress. But that is just what Schiff made Congress do after he saw what happened with

Mueller and the disaster that was. Mueller looked like a doddering old fool who didn't even know what was in the report
and that in effect ended all questions about Russian collusion. Schiff wasn't going to allow something like that to happen again.

Schiff shouldn't have even been running the proceedings.
He was chairman of the Intelligence Committee. Pelosi took
impeachment out of the hands of the Judiciary Committee,
where impeachment has always started, because she saw the
incompetence of Jerry Nadler running a hearing. Also, by
putting it with the Intelligence Committee, Schiff could do
it in secret and make all the rules. That is not representing
the people. That gave him the chance to leak out whatever he
wanted to the lemmings in the press and control the narrative.
He also shut down Republicans who wanted to ask questions
about the whistleblower.[24]

And let's not forget this so-called whistleblower, the person who started us all down this path to nowhere. Adam Schiff
decided you, the American people, didn't need to hear from
the whistleblower. You weren't to speak his name even though
everyone knew who he was, Eric Ciaramella, a CIA agent left
over from the Obama White House. His testimony had to be
conducted behind closed doors because he either lied in his
complaint describing the president's phone call or had nothing to do with writing the complaint in the first place. For all
we know, Shifty Schiff invented the complaint out of whole
cloth and simply attributed it to Ciaramella. Or maybe it was
just another "parody."

In high school I learned one of the principal tenets of
the freedom of our nation is the right to face your accuser. I

was taught as a child that in communist Russia, people could accuse you of things and you had no right to face your accuser or question him. And I was told as a child that that was what made America great. People couldn't falsely accuse you and hide.

Then, one day I woke up and learned Pelosi had introduced Soviet-style tactics to America. The whistleblower didn't want to come before Congress but wanted to testify in writing so he could stay completely hidden. We're talking about the impeachment of a President here and the chief witness wants to deny the president his right to face his accuser. This is the biggest decision a country can make, and all the evidence was gathered behind closed doors, out of sight. What was released was cherry-picked to make sure the story Pelosi wanted to tell was told.

So, the Democrats violated every basic principle of justice to try to remove a president who was fairly elected. They lied into the record right from their opening statement. They called witnesses who didn't witness anything. They broke long-standing norms on how impeachment hearings are conducted. And they denied the president his right to face his accuser. They made American justice look no better than that of the Soviets, the Castros, or Mao. I hope you haven't forgotten how many bodies piled up under them because these principles were abandoned.

The impeachment sham should have resulted in Schiff being thrown out of office. Public light showed what a fraud his star chamber was. The "witnesses" were not witness to anything and they only gave opinions about what they thought about the president's actions.

The truth is the Democrats had nothing but opinions being presented as facts on alleged behavior that is not even illegal, just "inappropriate." The "witnesses" were all exposed under questioning from Republicans. They offered nothing of probative value, only political value.

It's important to understand that the impeachment of President Trump was every bit the hoax Russiagate was because there will be more. If Donald Trump wins the election in November, you can bet the same discredited cheats and liars will be back to start the whole process over with a new scam.

THE MAIL-IN ELECTION THEFT

Of course, the Democrats won't have to nullify this year's election if they can manage to steal it for their senile candidate. This was already a huge concern before Covid-19, but just as they used that very real public health crisis to punish Republican voters and destroy the economy in an election year, they are also trying to use it to steal the 2020 presidential election.

The crazed governor of my state has already signed a bill to mail out a ballot to every registered voter in California.[25] That pretty much gives the election away to the Democrats, who will be mailing in these ballots for dead people, illegal aliens, and who knows who else. It probably doesn't matter quite as much in California, where the Democrat candidate is almost assured of victory, but that's not the case in other states. Besides, we conservatives in California would at least like to exercise our right to a fair election, win or lose.

I asked President Trump what he was doing about this when he appeared on my show, *The Savage Nation,* in June.

Well, we're suing, and we're filing another big lawsuit, I think on Friday. I think we have a good case. Newsom announced that he's sending out millions and millions of mail-in ballots. And, you know, you say, "Who are they sending these to?" And maybe who aren't. Let's say you take a Republican district and maybe those ballots don't get sent there. This is the craziest thing. This will be a rigged election if they're allowed to do it.[26]

The media dismiss the president's concerns as false and "debunked."[27] It's becoming a fairly reliable rule of thumb that when the liberal media claim something has been debunked, it's probably true. "Without evidence" is another bit of media propaganda created expressly for this president. For no former president do I recall supposed journalists writing, "The president claimed, without evidence . . ." Has any president ever carried around binders full of data to back up the claims they made?

The truth is voter fraud is a real problem. The White House official website lists many of the most prevalent forms of voter fraud and provides more than a thousand real examples taken from all fifty states. The types of voter fraud listed include:

IMPERSONATION FRAUD AT THE POLLS: Voting in the name of other legitimate voters and voters who have died, moved away, or lost their right to vote because they are felons, but remain registered.

FALSE REGISTRATIONS: Voting under fraudulent voter registrations that either use a phony name and a real or fake address or claim residence in a particular jurisdiction where the registered voter does not actually live and is not entitled to vote.

DUPLICATE VOTING: Registering in multiple locations and voting in the same election in more than one jurisdiction or state.

FRAUDULENT USE OF ABSENTEE BALLOTS: Requesting absentee ballots and voting without the knowledge of the actual voter; or obtaining the absentee ballot from a voter and either filling it in directly and forging the voter's signature or illegally telling the voter who to vote for.

BUYING VOTES: Paying voters to cast either an in-person or absentee ballot for a particular candidate.

ILLEGAL "ASSISTANCE" AT THE POLLS: Forcing or intimidating voters—particularly the elderly, disabled, illiterate, and those for whom English is a second language—to vote for particular candidates while supposedly providing them with "assistance."

INELIGIBLE VOTING: Illegal registration and voting by individuals who are not U.S. citizens, are convicted felons, or are otherwise not eligible to vote.

ALTERING THE VOTE COUNT: Changing the actual vote count either in a precinct or at the central location where votes are counted.

BALLOT PETITION FRAUD: Forging the signatures of registered voters on the ballot petitions that must be filed with election officials in some states for a candidate or issue to be listed on the official ballot.[28]

Now, just ask yourself how many of those types of voter fraud would be infinitely easier if every registered voter were mailed a ballot. Almost half of those people aren't intending to vote. Can any reasonable person believe a percentage of their ballots won't end up in the hands of vote fraudsters? I agree with the president that this may be the biggest risk he and the Republican Party face in this year's election.

California wasn't the first state to encourage widespread mail-in voting. At the time Governor Newsom signed the bill for California, five other states, Colorado, Hawaii, Oregon, Washington, and Utah, were already conducting their elections largely by mail-in votes.[29] The other forty-four states were roughly divided between those that allowed mail-in voting by request and those that required a compelling reason to allow the voter to mail in a vote instead of showing up at a polling place.

Those numbers could drastically change, especially if a new round of lockdowns is issued by governors reacting to reports, misleading or not, of new surges in Covid-19 cases. This would be just the excuse the cryptofascists need to get every state to consider mail-in voting. The CDC has its feet on both sides of the fence. As of this writing, they were giving recommendations for how to handle mail-in voting, but their website still contains this statement:

Mail-in voting can make it more difficult for voters with disabilities to exercise their right to vote. Election officials should ensure that accessible voting options are available and that these options are consistent with the recommendations for slowing the spread of COVID-19.[30]

You could take that statement one of two ways. It's encouraging that the agency acknowledges the importance of ensuring voters with disabilities can vote. But are they the only exception? The other recommendations as of late June largely assume people will be going to polling places to vote in person but watch out for this agency. It's still part of the Swamp, as it always has been, and could easily jump on board a national campaign to make all voting mail-in in 2020.

We have an enormous task in front of us. First, we need to get Donald Trump reelected. That in itself will be hard enough with all the dishonest, un-American, anticapitalist, anti-freedom forces aligned against us, given the air of legitimacy by the lying media. But simply putting Trump back in the White House will not be enough. I told you it wasn't enough in 2017. That's why I wrote *Trump's War*. Nothing about that has changed. It's only gotten worse.

Make no mistake, every new story, every new headline, every new accusation in an election year is designed for one thing and one thing only: the acquisition of power. It is not to find justice. It is to wear you down. It is to break you. The goal is not only for you to give up and stop supporting the president you voted for, but to accept the Establishment nullifying your vote even if he wins. They will not allow our agenda to be fully implemented while there is a breath of life left in them.

The Russians supposedly interfered in our election in 2016 by trying to foment discord among the American people using social media ads. Well, the Democrats are doing exactly what they accused the Russians of doing. They are sowing discord openly with riots and eroding social cohesion with lockdowns and mandatory mask orders. They have cynically exploited the coronavirus and the detestable murder of George Floyd for maximum political gain at our expense. Watch for them to try to steal the election with millions of fraudulent mail-in ballots and continue their violent revolution if they fail.

If the Democrats are allowed to succeed in this coup, our nation will become another Venezuela. The rule of law *must* be followed. It must be applied to both sides. The Adam Schiffs, Jerry Nadlers, and their allies in the Deep State must be brought to justice. The law applies to them, too, and they have all broken it in an attempt to nullify the 2016 election.

We are still a representative republic on paper. So was Rome during the years after Augustus, but everyone knows the republic was dead. Everyone voted in the Soviet Union; turnout was near 100 percent, as it was in the People's Republic of China under Mao. If we let these power-mad maniacs destroy the sanctity of the ballot box, we'll be no freer ourselves.

ELEVEN

NEOCONS AND RINOS ARE STILL AMONG US

In the councils of government, we must guard against the acquisition of unwarranted influence, whether sought or unsought, by the military-industrial complex. The potential for the disastrous rise of misplaced power exists and will persist.

We must never let the weight of this combination endanger our liberties or democratic processes. We should take nothing for granted. Only an alert and knowledgeable citizenry can compel the proper meshing of huge industrial and military machinery of defense with our peaceful methods and goals, so that security and liberty may prosper together."[1]

Those famous words were spoken by President Dwight D. Eisenhower, one of the great presidents of the twentieth century. He warned us about people like John Bolton and the generals who lined up to try to stick a knife in President Trump's back because he wants to end the disastrous foreign policy they've led—and profited from—for most of this century. Let's face it, most of the conservative media did nothing but cheerlead these neocons until Trump came to town. But when Bolton released his so-called insider's tell all book, everyone suddenly started making believe they were against him.

I, on the other hand, being someone even the president says has "street smarts," detested this slimeball right from the beginning. I warned the president about Bolton at Mar-a-Lago way back in December 2016, before the president was even sworn in. The president shooed everyone away and sat down and talked with me about quite a few things. One of the things we discussed that I am at liberty to divulge was my conversation about "the mustache."

Bolton was circling the buffet from the outer perimeter. We both saw this loser, this flop, this castaway, this bum, this nobody. He couldn't even get the leftover meatballs the help didn't want. The president asked my opinion about him and I said, "Watch out for this guy. He's a snake; he got us into Iraq." Unfortunately, the rest of Conservative Inc. lobbied for the bum and the rest is history.

So, it was no surprise to me when Bolton stabbed the president in the back with his book. Now, everyone knows that if you sign a nondisclosure agreement (NDA), you're bound by it, whether your job involves national security or not. If you sign an NDA and then violate it, you're going to be sued and lose a lot of money. Now, add to that the responsibility carried by someone who is allowed into the corridors of power, where major decisions are made about war and peace, life and death. You can't allow a vermin like this to repay that trust by publicly spreading lies and half-truths just for political and personal gain.

If there is a charge that can be levied for breaking the public trust like this, Bolton should have been arrested immediately and booked on it. As I said on Twitter just after he released his book,

BOLTON IS A TRAITOR! I TRIED TO WARN TRUMP IN DEC 2016. HE WAS ALWAYS A BRUTUS. SHOULD BE TRIED FOR TREASON[2]

I also publicly warned the inner circle at the White House to watch out for those who lobbied to have President Trump take Bolton in. They're the same as Bolton himself and always have been.

Honestly, the claims in Bolton's book don't amount to much when you really step back and analyze them.

Then there is the quisling Roberts. I'm talking about Chief Justice of the Supreme Court John Roberts, who once again sided with the Ginsburg wing of the Court. He's a Bushie, just like Bolton. The Bush dynasty is composed of very powerful people who have run America for generations. George W. Bush's grandfather, Prescott Bush, was a powerful U.S. senator. His son, George H. W. Bush, was a World War II pilot, head of the CIA, and later president. Then, his idiot son became president, marking the third generation of Bushes to wield power at the highest levels.

Well, they've always hated Donald Trump because he's an outsider. He was not part of the machine, not part of the system, and not part of the club. They tried to run Jeb Bush against him and Trump not only defeated Jeb in the primaries, he viciously humiliated him. He smeared the streets with poor Jeb and the Bush family never forgave him for it.

Not only does this wing of the Republican Establishment have personal reasons for hating the president, they have ideological reasons. From the moment Donald Trump made his first foreign policy speech back in 2016,[3] it was clear he was a threat not only to the far-left revolution that began under Obama, but to the neocon domination of the Republican Party that started with George W. Bush and continued right up until Donald Trump descended that escalator in 2015 and hit the party like a thunderbolt.

Donald Trump remains the key figure standing in the way of everything these people stand for. Let's not forget that the neoconservatives are basically liberals. The movement started when the warmonger wing of the Democrat Party got fed up with the party's antiwar direction and left to join the Republican Party. Their DNA is really liberal, which is why you find them supporting amnesty for illegal aliens and other left-wing causes whenever they can get away with it. Even their warmongering is based upon liberal thinking. They believe they can "transform" savage, alien cultures into Western-style democracies by dropping bombs on them. This springs from the same liberal delusion that human nature can be changed through government intervention here at home.

We also shouldn't forget that their worldview has been extremely lucrative for them over the years. My longtime listeners know I've always said, "Follow the money," and this is no exception. The Bush dynasty, Halliburton, the neocon think tanks, the defense contractors, and a whole host of tax-devouring merchants of death have something to lose if President Trump fully implements his America First foreign policy of peace through strength. Just look at who comes out of the woodwork to condemn the president whenever he tries to extricate us from some foreign boondoggle. Liberal Democrat generals like James Mattis and neocons like Bolton, Bill Kristol, and Max Boot are suddenly allies united against Trump.

So, you get this boll weevil Bolton, a Brutus, coming out of nowhere with his book during an election year. He was like a poison dart shot at the administration from the Bush dynasty blowpipe. Nobody heeded my warnings about this bum back when the Swamp was pitching him. I hope they'll listen to me now. The administration should take a little more advice from people who care about the survival of the nation.

This is the Bush family and all their neocon cohorts taking their revenge on Trump through the generals, through Bolton, through the media, the military-industrial complex, and finally the Supreme Court. Chief Justice Roberts spat in the president's face when he sided with the Ginsburg wing in basically saying Deferred Action for Childhood Arrivals (DACA) should be the law of the land.[4] I know many people were stunned, wondering how he could do such a thing. He didn't just spit in the president's face, he spat in the faces of every conservative in the country, those of us who not only want a wall on our border but an America inside it that still possesses borders, a language, and a culture of its own. He also sided with the extreme left on abortion in the Louisiana Act 620 case.[5]

A SOFT MILITARY COUP

In the midst of the left-wing assault on our civilization, we witnessed a soft military coup attempt against President Trump. One after another, generals, admirals, and other former prominent members of the military came out with sharply critical statements against President Trump. In all, the list includes seven generals, three admirals, and four former defense secretaries.[6] These included Generals James Mattis and John Kelly, both former members of Trump's own cabinet.

These all came on the heels of Trump's current defense secretary, Mark Esper, publicly breaking with Trump on using the military to quell the riots. Esper, by the way, has a strong military background. He saw action in the 1990–91 Gulf War with the "Screaming Eagles" as a member of the 101st Airborne and later commanded a rifle company in Italy. But after publicly contradicting his commander-in-chief on the use of the military against violent rioters, he did something even more unbelievable. Behind the president's back and without the president's concurrence, Esper disarmed the guardsmen in Washington, D.C., and sent home active-duty troops ordered there by President Trump.

So, the defense secretary decided these soldiers would face the bricks, the stones, the urine, the vomit, and the fists of these vermin in the streets unarmed. You have to ask yourself how a defense secretary with combat experience could send men into an urban battlefield and tell them not to use weapons or even to shoulder them. How did this nation devolve so rapidly before our eyes?

The whole nation saw the looting. All of us, including minorities, who know what's going on, want the National Guard to stop it. If they couldn't stop the looters and rioters, we wanted the military to do so. Instead, we saw the equivalent of a stand-down order. In fact, it was worse than that. Ordering the guardsmen to withdraw would be bad enough, but sending them into the streets in uniform, unarmed against an angry mob, is even worse.

So, I wasn't exaggerating when I said this was a soft military coup against the president. His direct orders were countermanded without his permission or even the courtesy of notification.

CRIMINAL REFORM INSTEAD OF POLICE REFORM

We keep hearing we need police reform. I disagree. I think we need criminal reform. Here in California, our radical left-wing governor released thousands of hardened criminals into the streets. First, it was part of "prison reform," whatever that means. Then, it was supposedly because of the Covid epidemic. How many of the thieves who broke windows and robbed stores had been among those released by this governor or his comrades in other states? We'll never know because the vermin in the press will never report it.

A friend of mine who fought the communists in Vietnam and has the shrapnel in his body to prove it wrote to me while this was going on. He is a graduate of one of America's most prestigious military academies and a registered military historian. He said what we see happening is an insurgency, part of a revolutionary movement. He said the tactics being employed are classic revolutionary strategy, which includes undermining the authority and credibility of the government, sowing fear and distrust among the population, and subverting the means of communication in the media. He said the left would go all out to subvert the November election by any means.

Another common revolutionary tactic is to use the tempo of the action to rob banks for the money to fund further operations. We saw one of the Left's foot soldiers die when an explosive he was using on an ATM went off in his face. Several other ATMs were hit in the same city that day.

My friend also expressed concern about the behavior of the generals and defense secretary. Why would they put out statements saying the president doesn't have authority to deploy troops for civil disturbances unless the generals are part of the opposition? They knew their statements would be broadcast uncritically by the anti-Trump media.

In case anyone missed the Bush dynasty connection in this whole soft military coup, Colin Powell came out of the woodwork to side with his fellow former generals against the president.[7] He didn't just criticize the president considering using the military to protect us from the street thugs. He also confirmed he would be voting for Sleepy Joe Biden in November. That's not really news. After playing a major role in getting us into he disastrous Iraq War under Republican president George W. Bush, he threw his support to Obama in subsequent elections. So, he's been on the wrong side of everything for this entire century.

ARE AMERICANS ALLOWED TO DREAM ANYMORE?

We in America are now beaten up and passive. We're letting street thugs dictate our lives on every level. I'd like to tell you that American dreamers dream first. I realize that Justice Roberts and Nancy Pelosi have DREAMers and that the church has DREAMers. But what happened to we, the American people, and our dream to make America great again?

I maintain that American dreamers, those born here and those legally naturalized, have the right to dream first and we have an obligation to encourage them to do so. Dreams by Americans plant seeds that grow and nourish America. We are the real dreamers and we're far more numerous than the interlopers and invaders. We, the American people who voted for Donald Trump, are the real dreamers. We have a vision of our nation, strong and unified, not for this minority or that special interest group, but for all. That is the heart of our Declaration of Independence. We have a dream to make America great again.

Do you even remember what your own dream is? Do you remember the promises that were made? They're all in my book, *Trump's War*. We dreamed of a nation that defended its borders, language, and culture. We hoped for leaders who would be fiscally conservative and restore our way of life, eroded for decades by the progressives.

Now, of course, Pelosi and Schumer parade a selected group of DREAMers before the American people. They only want you to see the few that are service members or college students. But please keep in mind that only nine hundred of the DACA beneficiaries were serving in the military when Trump first attempted to undo Obama's "pen and phone" order.[8] And while the left paints a picture that the rest of them are studious high school students, many are actually adults.

According to the left-leaning Pew Research Center,

> The average age of "Dreamers" enrolled in DACA is 24 years old. Those 25 and younger make up two-thirds of active DACA recipients—29% are ages 16–20 and 37% are ages 21–25. About a quarter (24%) are ages 26–30, while one-in-ten (11%) are ages 31–36.[9]

Only 49 percent of DACA beneficiaries have received a high school diploma. The Department of Homeland Security reported in 2017 that 2,139 DACA beneficiaries had their status revoked for criminal activity.[10] So, perhaps the image of the average DACA beneficiary as an all-American high school student toting a book bag on the way to school and staying late for marching band practice is a bit misleading.

While the image Democrats portray of DACA beneficiaries is a lie, the real reason DACA should end immediately is it is unconstitutional. This was an executive order written by President Obama that made official his policy of violating the oath he took to "take care that the laws are faithfully executed." That is the primary duty of the president, as head of the executive branch, to *execute* the laws. President Trump gave Congress every opportunity to rectify the situation with legislation. No court in the land should be forcing him to break his own oath by prohibiting him from performing that duty.

The Department of Homeland Security issued its own statement on this constitutional travesty:

Acting Secretary Chad Wolf: "DACA recipients deserve closure and finality surrounding their status here in the U.S. Unfortunately, today's Supreme Court decision fails to provide that certainty. The DACA program was created out of thin air and implemented illegally. The American people deserve to have the Nation's laws faithfully executed as written by their representatives in Congress—not based on the arbitrary decisions of a past Administration. This ruling usurps the clear authority of the Executive Branch to end unlawful programs."

Acting Deputy Secretary Ken Cuccinelli: "The Supreme Court's decision is an affront to the rule of law and gives Presidents power to extend discretionary policies into future Administrations. No Justice will say that the DACA program is lawful, and that should be enough reason to end it. Justice Clarence Thomas had it right in dissent: 'Such timidity [by SCOTUS] forsakes the Court's duty to apply the law according to neutral principles and the ripple effects of the majority's error will be felt throughout our system of self-government.'"[11]

Do you remember when the Republicans used to bloviate about the Constitution and the rule of law? Some still do, but the Establishment Republicans outnumber them. We sent real

conservatives to Congress in 2010 and 2012, but let's not forget who the presidential nominee was in 2012. He's currently
marching with the communists in Black Lives Matter.[12] He's
probably only doing it to signal his opposition to the president and maybe he's ignorant of the fact that this organization is run by Marxists. But does it really matter? He's helping
to empower an ideology that led to people just like him being
executed in countries where it became mainstream.

The overwhelming majority of Republican *voters* still support President Trump.[13] His support in the Congress appears
to mirror that but I'm warning you now to not take that political support for granted. I don't trust half the Republicans
in Congress. Some are true conservatives who believe in the
same things we do. We should know; we helped get them
elected. But others have only supported the president to keep
their seats, knowing opposing him while the economy was
riding high and the country was on the right track was political suicide. There is some percentage of these Republicans
who are RINOs and will turn around and stab the president
in the back at the first sign of weakness.

The neocons and RINOs may have lost a huge battle in
2016 after President Trump annihilated their candidate, Jeb
Bush. But the war against them isn't over. Just as they did in
2016, these liberals in conservative clothing won't hesitate to
support the Democrat candidate. They are already organizing and raising funds for Sleepy Joe as of this writing and they
will be out in full force as Election Day nears.[14] "If you don't
vote for Trump that's a victory but if you're actively supporting Biden, that's a huge victory. That's a-two vote difference,"
said one of the Judases.[15] The Lincoln Project and Right Side

PAC may not represent the majority of Republicans, but they don't need to. All they need to do is whittle away a few million votes here and there to swing the election.

Let's not forget that the conservative base is not enough for Donald Trump to win. He won in 2016 by getting votes from significant numbers of independent voters, even people who voted for Obama in 2012. He won some traditionally blue states by razor-thin margins that could go either way this November. All the fake conservative Republicans need to do is influence a small percentage of those votes to go the other way and we are looking at a Biden presidency.

We must be on our guard against turncoats in the Republican Party. I warned about them in my 2017 book, *Trump's War*, and nothing has changed. They are still there, like termites trying to rot the Republican Party from within. Our battle to extricate them from the tree of liberty continues.

TWELVE

STARING INTO THE ABYSS

FROM THE FRENCH REVOLUTION TO THE AMERICAN LEFTIST REVOLUTION, FROM CLIMATE HYSTERIA TO RACIAL HYSTERIA

America is on the precipice of an abyss. We are staring into a self-made oblivion where everything that has previously defined the greatest nation in human history is erased. Rather than fighting with our last breath to avoid it, we are running headlong into the chasm, like lemmings stampeding over a cliff. As Dostoyevsky wrote, "When I fall into the abyss, I go straight into it, head down and heels up, and I'm even pleased that I'm falling in just such a humiliating position, and for me I find it beautiful."[1]

One thing is certain: once we fall in ourselves, we won't find it beautiful. We will be reliving the nightmare so many populations have lived before us, all promised a utopia free from the "oppression" of capitalism and the nuclear family. And if the radicals have their way, it will be hard to find our way back, our history having been erased by the American Red Guards toppling statues and renaming universities, streets, and other landmarks.

Some may wonder how we got here. That's no mystery. It started with radical feminists, the free love movement, and the rise of the radical left in the 1960s. We stood by and dismissed it as a fringe movement. We comforted ourselves with the idea we still had law and order to put them down. Then, in the 1990s, we elected one of those left-wing radicals president, Bill Clinton. America saw what it did and in 1994 elected a conservative Republican Congress to counter the communist in disguise for the moment. But all the while, the subversion taking place in higher education, on TV, in the movies, and in the news continued. And still we looked away because we were a nation of law and order and love of country.

After coming together briefly as a nation and a society after 9/11, the subversion resumed in the same stealth fashion. We elected the first black president even though we could see he was a naked communist. He was mentored by the noted communist Frank Marshall Davis as a young man and attended a church steeped in black liberation theology. He befriended known anti-American terrorist Bill Ayers.

As he divided the country racially, allowed states and cities to ignore immigration laws, and had his attorney general conduct a war on police, we looked away because we still believed law and order and our Constitution would protect us. Meanwhile, the subversion lurking just beneath the surface was about to explode like a volcano.

Then we elected Donald Trump, a man who loved his country, loved the flag, loved law and order, respected our borders, and was committed to draining the Swamp. That's when all the elements of subversion that had been put into place erupted in a gusher of resistance. Masked radicals and anarchists shut down conservative speakers on college campuses. They broke windows and burned buildings with impunity. Mayors and governors openly flouted our borders, creating "sanctuary cities" and states. Religion was openly mocked and rejected. The FBI and CIA colluded to stop the Trump administration from functioning, concocting a phony Russia scandal that carried on for three years, disabling his efforts to move forward his agenda—our agenda.

Now these subversives have emerged in full force, using the death of a black man as their shield. They've made a seamless move from climate hysteria to racial hysteria based on the myth of racial injustice 155 years after the end of the Civil War and a half century after the 1964 Civil Rights Act. These fascists are tearing down statues, burning down or taking over parts of major American cities, and viciously beating people because of the color of their skin. God help you if you do not kneel to them or say the exact right words, because they will make sure you lose your job and any ability to support your family.

Like Mao's Red Guards, they seek to destroy statues and other physical evidence of America's previous history. But what statues will they erect in this newfound utopia? Karl Marx? Nelson Mandela? Will every statue be an MLK statue?

If American culture is to be erased, what will they replace it with? African culture? Meso-American culture? Let me remind you that all these cultures also held slaves, some of which were brutally sacrificed to their gods.

People are being forced to sit on company conference calls discussing what white people can do to apologize for and make up for their privilege. Governor Cuomo is telling us what a wonderful thing it is that these statues are being torn down. A Michigan mayor has resigned amid criticism for saying she'd be "crucified" if she didn't vote to reappoint a black city official. Police chiefs are resigning after officers shoot people. The word "chief" is being considered for removal from titles like "police chief" and "fire chief" in some cities.

A MARXIST BY ANY OTHER NAME

As we have shown in this book, what began as a legitimate protest against the murder by a deranged, homicidal officer of a black man who was shackled on the ground and crying for his mother, soon thereafter morphed into a full-blown, Marxist-revolutionary action. Black Lives Matter is a well-known Marxist front group, even admittedly so by its founders. They are just one of many of the snakes that have undermined this nation and threatened to turn us into Venezuela or worse.

In a previous book, *Scorched Earth*, I listed all the left-wing groups that are complicit in this long march toward Marxism. Antifa is the military wing of this long list of supposedly peaceful progressive organizations. They include Black Lives Matter, Antifa, Media Matters, the ACLU, and a host of other subversive groups bent on destroying America as a land of freedom and opportunity and replacing it with their radical socialist vision. I have a comprehensive list of these organizations in an appendix at the end of this book.

As I was finishing the manuscript for this book, Black Lives Matter marched into Beverly Hills chanting, "Eat the rich!" and "Abolish capitalism now!"[2] The national media reaction? There wasn't one. If conservatives march or rally in support of the right to bear arms or simply the right to go out and earn a living, they are immediately demonized as racists and "white supremacists," based on some tiny minority carrying Confederate flags or other banned paraphernalia. But leftists chanting the slogans of regimes that killed hundreds of millions—orders of magnitude more than the total number of slaves who ever lived in America—are not worthy of mention.

What little coverage there was by local media of this overtly Marxist rally criticized the police for arresting twenty-eight of the "protestors," including one suspected of arson.[3] As fellow communist Greta Dumberg would say, "How dare they?"

In a fitting tribute to the progenitor of modern leftism, the French Revolution, so-called protestors set up a guillotine in front of Jeff Bezos's Washington, D.C., residence.[4] Every tactic we're seeing today has been used previously by communist revolutions and they all got their inspiration from the bloody French Revolution.

The destroying of statues and other historical landmarks by Black Lives Matter, Antifa, and other left-wing groups is no exception. The French revolutionaries sought to erase all French history preceding the revolution. They instituted a new calendar and proclaimed 1792 "Year 1." The Khmer Rouge in Cambodia similarly designated 1975 to be "Year Zero." That was part of the inspiration for my previous *New York Times* bestseller, *Government Zero*.

During the early years of the Bolshevik Revolution in Russia, statues of the Romanovs were destroyed, followed by the Romanovs themselves. Never forget that those who would pull down statues will eventually pull down the people, too. I hope Jeff Bezos is getting the message. He'd better start fighting on the right side.

The playbook never changes for these enemies of civilization. First, it's erase the past. Then, it's "eat the rich," meaning seize all their property, killing anyone who resists. Then, it's absolute rule by a few, wealthy party elites and subjugation, poverty, and slavery for everyone else. Do you think it can't happen here? Look around. It is happening here, right before your eyes.

LOCKDOWN II

As I said in a previous chapter and will continue to emphasize, I never believed the coronavirus itself was a deliberate attack or a left-wing hoax. Until I see compelling evidence to the contrary, I will stick with my initial assessment that this was a virus that escaped a Chinese laboratory by accident after having been manipulated artificially, either to develop a new bioweapon or a new vaccine. Scientists manipulate viruses for both reasons all the time.

However, while the virus itself was not a hoax or a politically motivated attack, almost the entire reaction to it was a combination of both. There were a number of ways governments could have responded to the virus, including the right way, selective quarantine of the most at-risk populations.

The proper response was too politically incorrect for cowardly politicians to even consider, as it would have meant locking down all the most popular victim groups. Just take a look at where the concentration of deaths from the virus occurred: in nursing homes, large urban centers dominated by homeless bums, illegal aliens, and poor minorities. We were reminded that "people of color" were disproportionately dying or becoming seriously ill from the virus. Black Medicare patients, for example, were four times as likely to be hospitalized after contracting the virus as white Medicare patients.[5]

This must have been the result of "white privilege" or the legacy of slavery, we were led to believe. Certainly, it is forbidden to suggest that perhaps diet or other lifestyle choices rendered some populations more susceptible to becoming sick or even that dense urban centers, where all epidemics of history have been concentrated, may be affected differently than rural or suburban areas.

Instead of selective quarantine, power mad, left-wing governors decided to take the unprecedented step of locking whole populations in their homes, the healthy along with the sick, and closed down all businesses they in their completely valueless opinions deemed "nonessential."

Now, while this was never a good idea from a public health perspective or otherwise, perhaps it could have been written off as panic or poor judgment early in the crisis, when little was known about the virus or its mortality rate. But as time went on and it became apparent that states or countries without lockdowns were faring no worse, in fact often better, than the states or countries with the strictest policies, there was no excuse to keep whole populations under what amounted to virtual house arrest.

We now know the lockdowns not only didn't work; they probably made the problem worse. Blue states were hit much harder than red states in terms of deaths per million.[6] States with lockdowns also had a mortality rate *four times higher* than states that didn't lock down at all![7]

Almost half of all Covid-19 deaths nationwide were people in nursing homes, the hardest hit residing in New York, New Jersey, Massachusetts, and Pennsylvania.[8] These were the most locked-down populations of all, with most states banning visitors from coming in or residents from leaving their facilities. Yet, almost half the deaths were nursing home residents.

Of course, New York tops the list thanks to Governor "Sausage and Peppers" Cuomo ordering nursing homes to accept patients who had tested positive for Covid-19 at the hospital.[9]

Yet, despite all this clear and compelling evidence that lockdowns don't work and may have made the problem worse, governors around the country are preparing their populations for yet another round of lockdowns over a supposed spike in "cases" in recently reopened states. This is pure propaganda to win support for another attack on our economy and way of life.

Do you remember "two weeks to flatten the curve"? That's what we were told when the first lockdowns were imposed back in March.[10] It seems like ancient history now, but that original justification for the lockdowns was to prevent too many hospitalizations from occurring at once and thereby "overwhelming the hospitals."

Hospitals in general were never overwhelmed, not even at the peak of the crisis. That should have meant the end of the lockdowns, even by the public health officials' faulty reasoning, since the stated purpose was never to limit the amount of total cases. But then, there was a new reason to continue them. "Covid-19 can be spread by asymptomatic people!" screamed headlines. A study came out appearing to confirm that and Dr. Slouchy, the Sorcerer's Apprentice, said it "lays the question to rest."

Well, that study turned out to be based on a single case and upon further scrutiny, it turned out the supposedly "asymptomatic" woman who infected four other people did have symptoms at the time but no one had ever interviewed her! The study Slouchy had said laid the question to rest was retracted by *Science* on February 3, long before any lockdowns were imposed.[11]

More studies were done, all of which failed to confirm a single case of Covid-19 being spread by asymptomatic people. A later study published on May 8 concluded that "transmission from asymptomatic, rather than presymptomatic, individuals is not a major driver of spread."[12]

The truth is scientists don't know for sure that Covid-19 can be spread by asymptomatic people but suspect it can be due to the high number of cases of people who have minor or no symptoms. This is very similar to the current scientific consensus on whether influenza can be spread by asymptomatic people. Scientists suspect it can be spread that way, but it is difficult to confirm a case.

The real dishonesty here was in representing the possibility of asymptomatic spread as something unique to Covid-19 and firmly established by scientific research. It wasn't. As a scientist myself, I view this as an open question awaiting more definitive proof. I tend to think the last study I cited is probably correct: spread by asymptomatic people is probable but not a significant part of the spread of the virus. Sometimes you must apply a little common sense to the data. Does anyone really believe an asymptomatic person who is positive for the virus is spreading it anywhere near the rate someone who is coughing and wheezing is spreading it? Of course not.

So, the prospect of asymptomatic people spreading the virus was never a valid reason to lock all of society down, either. Certainly, by early May, when we had a lot more information on this subject than we did in February or March, those policies should have been discontinued. They weren't.

As I prepare to turn this manuscript into the publisher, headlines are blaring with a supposed new outbreak of the virus. States that aggressively reopened, we are told, are "paying the price" with an explosion of new cases. NPR assures us this is 100 percent the result of conservatives exercising their rights and zero percent because of the riots in late May and early June.[13] There is no limit to the absurdity liberal media is willing to peddle and liberal voters are willing to believe.

What is glaringly missing from every headline and every "news" report is the weekly Covid-19 death count. That should give any reasonable person pause. Why were we accosted with nothing but headlines on Covid-19 deaths in April but now only told about new "cases"? Answer: Covid-19 deaths peaked in April and declined every week thereafter.[14] The explosion in new cases is merely the result of more widespread testing, which is confirming what we already knew. Covid-19 is not an issue for most healthy, working-age people.

Yet, these snakes in public health institutions and their insane, left-wing coconspirator governors are preparing to lock America down once again, if not during the summer then at least at the outset of the next flu season, which conveniently begins right before the election. Employing the same strategy in October 2020, armed with so much more information, as was employed in March 2020 is nothing but naked political opportunism at every American's expense.

Watch for another round of "protests" against racism, too, just before the election. The left has gone from Lloyd George to George Floyd. Lloyd George, an extreme liberal but a patriot, used to be a hero for the left. Now it is George Floyd, a criminal who did not deserve to die for the crime he committed, but was a career criminal nonetheless. He was given a mass funeral usually reserved for heads of state or captains of industry, while everyday Americans were not allowed to hold Christian burials or funerals for their dead. This is just more evidence the lockdowns are entirely political.

When the media is scolding any conservative who dares to challenge the next wave of lockdowns while defending the next round of riots, looting, and destruction of private property, any American still possessing the ability to reason will know this has nothing to do with a virus and everything to do with a Marxist revolution. The only question then will be what can be done to defeat it.

That's assuming it can be defeated. Pat Buchanan asked, "Have the mobs won?" in an article in early July.[15] I know the president is very big on rhetoric and tweeting, but apparently the vandals and barbarians are not going to be arrested and stopped.

Meanwhile, Governor Newsolini of California banned singing and chanting in churches and houses of worship. I couldn't believe it when I first saw the news report. We're not living in China, North Korea, or Iraq under Saddam Hussein.

Now, understand that Governor Newsom is backed by the most phenomenally radical people in the history of the state of California. They're hard-core Stalinists. They hate religion, as all Marxists do. And just as in the ex–Soviet Union, the church became their enemy.

I had never seen anything like this. No other governor in history, no American politician whatsoever, would have dared do this. You had tens of thousands of barbarians and vandals gathering outdoors in cities across the state of California screaming and chanting. There was not one word from Governor Newsom. Yet, the churches were told to stop singing and chanting?

For a moment, I thought I was alone, until faith leaders came out and slammed this dictator's edict. Sean Feucht, a pastor in northern California, has started a "Let Us Worship" petition. He compared Newsom to Pharaoh of Exodus on his website, reading the verse from Exodus that says, "This is what the Lord says, 'Let my people go, so that they may worship me.'"[16]

Pastor Les Simmons of the South Sacramento Christian Center told KCRA, "In particular, the Black culture, singing in churches goes all the way back from 400 years ago during slavery up until now. Singing was our thing that got us through."[17] So, a black pastor stood up to Governor Newsolini, although I saw nothing from the mosques and nothing from the synagogues.

This is an important story in that it shows how power mad these governors are. The police have been neutralized by the vandals and barbarians and the verminous scum in the press and legal professions, the worthless worms, these coelenterates, say nothing. Governor Newsolini says nothing, but instead takes his venom out on poor, meek Christians, telling them they can't sing or chant.

It's astounding to me how weak we've become as a nation. We're weak from top to bottom, with no leadership. New York City was rendered a war zone after the police there were disarmed and deballed. Shootings in June of this year were higher than during any month since 1996. The mayor of New York, Bill de Blasio, didn't blame the thugs, or the barbarians, the leftist communists who are behind it. No, mentally ill de Blasio blamed the virus.[18] The people of New York got the mayor they deserved.

Years ago, I wrote a book called *Liberalism Is a Mental Disorder*. It wasn't written tongue-in-cheek. It was written as prophecy. A so-called botanist in London, England, said that plants, collected plants, and fungi are racist. They hired a Third Worlder to work in the great Kew Gardens of London and the first thing he did was pronounce plant collections racist.[19]

How in the world can America survive with Wolf Blitzer, Jake Tapper, and all the other communists in the media? I call them what they are. They may as well be working for the Communist Party USA with what they are doing to this incredible nation.

There are many men who are at their breaking point. I've met some myself. They are ready to snap and don't know who to strike out at. They're holding their fire and keeping their powder dry right now, but I will tell you this: they need to see something done about the destruction of their country. They want action, not just rhetoric and tweets.

Some say it's the governors who need to act. I've said myself that Trump shouldn't "take the bait," meaning use the military to quell the riots, because if he did he'd be called a dictator. I said he was between a rock and a hard place.

Well, guess what? I'm not a leader. Leaders are supposed to be smarter than talk show hosts. They have legions of the smartest people on earth around them. I don't. I'm a man alone in a room with an old, blind dog. I'm an immigrant's son living through a communist revolution right in my own nation with the vandals and barbarians as the street armies of the night.

We are living in unprecedented times. I lived through the civil rights movement. I lived through the killings at Kent State and the Vietnam War protests, but I have never lived through an outright, overt, naked communist revolution. We have vermin knocking over all the iconic statues of America with impunity. First they softened up the police. Once the police were neutralized, the mobs went after the symbols of America.

They're so crazy they knocked over a statue of Frederick Douglass, an African American hero who was born a slave but rose to become one of the preeminent orators and statesmen of his day.[20] Obviously, that showed this isn't about slavery or racism. It's about destroying the United States of America. It comes down to a simple phrase from the radical feminist who started it all: "Bring it all down, man."

Any statue of any man is a target now. Do you remember that other famous chant from the 1960s, "Hey, hey, ho, ho, Western Civ has got to go?" Let me tell you something. All the good liberals in Berkeley, sitting in their pompous little hills, are sitting ducks. These barbarians could run them over and nobody will help them. The cops you helped neutralize aren't there anymore. So, when the hordes come up the hills of Oakland, Berkeley, and all of East Bay, there won't be anyone for them to call. They neutralized the thin blue line because liberalism is a mental disorder.

So, I turn to my president, who I still pray will step into the breach and save the nation. I'm still voting for Donald Trump, because the alternative is dismal. But I'm different from most people. Many won't vote at all. In 2015, I said to the millions who had not voted because they knew it was all a crock of garbage, "I know you haven't voted in several elections because you know that no matter who gets elected, you get the same garbage. But please go out and vote because your vote matters."

Those people who decided to vote were the razor-thin margin that swung the Electoral College and put President Trump in the White House. I am speaking to those people again. Many have said they aren't voting for Trump. They aren't voting for Biden, either. They're just not voting. Don't think I don't hear it.

There are millions of armed men in America, ex-military, current military, ex-police, current police. They're armed to the teeth and they're boiling over with rage because they see nobody stepping into the breach. There is no such thing as a peaceful protestor anymore. These are not protestors. They're the street military arm of a revolution.

That little college girl marching with her girlfriend in the street just loves the thugs who break the windows. She really enjoys seeing the thugs and barbarians pelting the police with rocks and Molotov cocktails. They're all one and the same. This is no longer peaceable assembly as guaranteed to Americans in the First Amendment. When you have a mob that contains within it the seeds of violence and destruction, that mob no longer comprises a "peaceful protest."

The military has turned on President Trump. The generals did a Ten Days in May job on him. They've basically told him he's alone. They've told him he's not using the military for domestic disturbances. They've said there is no precedent for it, which is a lie. The military has been used to quell riots many times since 1957, when President Eisenhower called out the 101st Airborne to enforce the Supreme Court's famous *Brown v. Board of Education* ruling. More recently, President George H. W. Bush sent federal troops into Los Angeles to quell the 1992 riots.[21]

I believe the president should also explore the possibility of prosecuting street gangs who have extorted local businesses under the Racketeer Influenced and Corrupt Organizations Act (RICO). Claiming you're a victim of oppression doesn't give you a license to commit crimes against innocent people. These left-wing agitators have become organized street gangs and if they are using threats of violence or destruction to coerce corporations to support them or just plain shaking down local store owners for money or free merchandise, they should be prosecuted like any other criminal organization.

MORE THAN REELECTING TRUMP

The only thing that could stop the street violence and revolutionary actions against our heritage would be a foreign attack on our soil. God forbid this should happen, but our enemies are watching us very closely. They see the dissention in the streets. They see the nation is about to topple like the statues of its founders, George Washington and Thomas Jefferson. The underpinnings of our democracy themselves are being uprooted by the radical left.

Our foreign enemies see this. Let's hope they don't strike, but if they did, all the street agitators would be nullified. They would be stopped not by martial law but the popular will. Even the rats in the media would have to stop chewing at the base of the Statue of Liberty. We would all be united against our common enemy. It's a horrifying thought and let's hope it doesn't happen, but it could happen here.

Should we succeed in reelecting this administration, then the full force of these leftist organizations will be seen. The riots of the spring of 2020 will be meek compared to what will happen. Nevertheless, we must encourage our friends to vote and not give up hope. Every vote will count, especially on our side.

In the remote possibility that we succeed in heading off this revolution, our work will then begin. After the inauguration in 2021, we will have to go to war. We must force Congress— our Congress—to convene a new House Committee on Patriotism. In the 1950s, there was a House Committee on

Un-American Activities. It was 100 percent correct in trying to root out communism and communists in Hollywood, the media, and academia. Even then, it was besmirched by falsehoods like those used today.

However, the Venona Papers, published in the 1990s, the work of a former Soviet operative, confirmed Senator Joe McCarthy and HUAC were 100 percent correct. The communists had in fact secretly infiltrated Hollywood, academia, and the press. McCarthy was right, but he was hounded and destroyed by the media and left-wing operatives.

Therefore, we cannot call this new House committee by the same name. It would not work this time. We must call it the House Committee on Patriotism and it will have its work cut out for it. It will have to dispassionately investigate and eventually prove that all the groups listed here and those yet to be discovered are working secretly to undermine our republic. This is a monumental battle, but one we Americans are prepared to fight.

The grandfathers of today's Eddies, themselves ordinary men, took on the "supermen" and defeated Hitler. We, their descendants, can do the same to save our nation.

LEFT-WING ORGANIZATIONS WORTHY OF INVESTIGATION BY A HOUSE COMMITTEE ON PATRIOTISM

Alliance for Democracy; Amnesty International; Black Lives Matter; Center for American Progress; Center for Media and Democracy; Center for Science and the Public Interest; Citizens for Responsibility and Ethics in Washington; Citizen Action; Citizens Fund, ColorOfChange.org; Common Assets Defense Fund; Cordoba Initiative; Media Matters for America; MoveOn.org; ProPublica (funded by Soros); Netroots Nation; Tide Center; Tide Center Projects; Tides Foundation; Transnational Resource and Action Center; Turning Point Project; Youth Empowerment Center; Advancement Project; All of Us or None; Alliance for Justice; America Coming Together; America Votes; America's Voice; American Bar Association Commission on Immigration; American Bridge 21st Century; ACLU; American Constitution Society for Law and Policy; American Family Voices; Rockefeller Brothers

Fund; Lilly Endowment; Bain Foundation; Ford Foundation; Rockefeller Foundation; Blue Moon Fund; Joyce Foundation; HKH Foundation; Dolan Charitable Trust; Vanguard Foundation; Archer Foundation; Saul Alinsky's Back of the Yards Community Council; National Hip Hop Political Convention; Cuban Council of Churches; Pastors for Peace; Progressive Religious Partnership; People for the American Way; Interfaith Alliance; Interfaith Worker Justice; American Friends Service Committee; Clergy Leadership Network; America Coming Together; National Council of Churches; Interfaith Center on Corporate Responsibility.

CHAPTER 1: THE TWIN PLAGUES: COVIDISM AND COMMUNISM

1. "Full footage of George Floyd crying for his mother while being killed by police officer," YouTube. https://www.youtube.com/watch?v=PxIlWadqFQg&bpctr=1591546499.

2. Jonathan Neaman Lipman and Stevan Harrell, *Violence in China: Essays in Culture and Counterculture* (Albany: State University of New York Press, 1990), 154.

3. David Aaro, "Massachusetts police chief seen lying face down on pavement alongside protesters in show of solidarity," Fox News, June 8, 2020, https://www.foxnews.com/us/massachusetts-police-chief-lays-down-in-pavement-show-solidarity-protesters.

4. https://blacklivesmatter.com/what-we-believe/.

5. TED Personal Profile, Opal Tometi, https://www.ted.com/speakers/opal_tometi.

6. Robert Wenzel, "Some Background on the Black Lives Matter Organization," Target Liberty, June 7, 2020, https://www.targetliberty.com/2020/06/some-background-on-black-lives-matter.html.

7. Ibid.

8. Joshua Rhett Miller, "How Black Lives Matter Activists See the Future of Urban Policing," June 8, 2020, https://nypost.com/2020/06/08/how-black-lives-matter-activists-see-the-future-of-urban-policing/.

9. "Activists Investigate the History of Relationships of MPD with African Americans," *All Things Considered*, NPR, May 29, 2020, https://www.npr.org/2020/05/29/865685697/activists-investigate-the-history-of-relationships-of-mpd-with-african-americans.

10. https://blacklivesmatter.com/black-lives-matter-leads-coalition-to-free21savage/.

11. Alicia Wallace. "Shake Shack, Ruth's Chris and Other Chain Restaurants Got Big PPP Loans When Small Businesses Couldn't," CNN, April 20, 2020, https://www.cnn.com/2020/04/19/business/small-businesses-ppp-loans-chain-restaurants/index.html.

12. Kenneth Garger, "California Will Pay Illegal Immigrants Not Included in Coronavirus Stimulus," *New York Post,* April 16, 2020, https://nypost.com/2020/04/16/ca-to-pay-illegals-not-included-in-coronavirus-stimulus/.

13. Tim Worstall, "If You're Anti-Poverty You Should Be Pro–Free Trade and Globalization," *Forbes*, April 15, 2015, https://www.forbes.com/sites/timworstall/2015/10/01/if-youre-anti-poverty-you-should-be-pro-free-trade-and-globalisation/#7bbeb1a71d62.

14. Barnini Chakraborty, "China Hints at Denying Americans Life-saving Coronavirus Drugs," Fox News, March 13, 2020, https://www.foxnews.com/world/chinese-deny-americans-coronavirus-drugs.

15. Nikos Axarlis, "Plague Victims Found: Mass Burial in Athens," *Archaeology,* April 15, 1998, https://archive.archaeology.org/online/news/kerameikos.html.

16. The Editors, "Pandemics That Changed History," History, April 1, 2020, https://www.history.com/topics/middle-ages/pandemics-timeline.

17. "Bubonic Plague," Khan Academy, https://www.khanacademy.org/humanities/world-history/medieval-times/disease-and-demography/a/disease-and-demograpy.

18. William McNeill, *Plagues and Peoples* (New York: Anchor Books, 1977), 149.

CHAPTER 2: THE VIRUS PROFITEERS

1. Deroy Murdoch, "Deroy Murdock: Padding Coronavirus Stimulus Package with Pork Angers This John Kennedy," Fox News, March 31, 2020, https://www.foxnews.com/opinion/deroy-murdock-padding-coronavirus-stimulus-package-with-pork-angers-this-john-kennedy.

2. Stephen Moore, "Democrats Rooting for Recession," *Washington Times,* August 25, 2019. https://www.washingtontimes.com/news/2019/aug/25/rooting-recession/.

3. "Voting in America: A Look at the 2016 Presidential Election," U.S. Census Bureau, May 10, 2017, https://www.census.gov/newsroom/blogs/random-samplings/2017/05/voting_in_america.html.

4. Gregg Re, "AOC Celebrates Oil Crash in Now-Deleted Tweet: 'You Absolutely Love to See It.'"

5. "Cases, Hospitalizations and Deaths," NYC Health, April 26, 2020, https://www1.nyc.gov/site/doh/covid/covid-19-data.page.

6. Ibid.

7. Ashley Collman, "Navy Hospital Ship Comfort Is Leaving NYC After Treating Just 179 Patients in 3 Weeks," *Business Insider*, April 26, 2020, https://www.businessinsider.com/usns-comfort-nyc-coronavirus-timeline-2020-4.

8. Elizabeth Rosner and Natalie Musumeci, "An Inside Look at Central Park's Makeshift Coronavirus Hospital," *New York Post*, April 9, 2020, https://

nypost.com/2020/04/09/central-park-coronavirus-field-hospital-near-
capacity/.

9. Shane Harris, Justin Sondel, and Gregory S. Schneider, "Cash-Starved
Hospitals and Doctor Groups Cut Staff Amid Pandemic," *Washington
Post*, April 9, 2020, https://www.washingtonpost.com/health/starved-for-
cash-hospitals-and-doctor-groups-cut-staff-amid-pandemic/2020/04/09/
d3593f54-79a7-11ea-a130-df573469f094_story.html.

10. Annika Merrilees, "Rural Hospitals, Without Coronavirus Patients, See
Empty Beds and Dark Hallways Instead," *St. Louis Post-Dispatch,* May
2, 2020, https://www.stltoday.com/business/local/rural-hospitals-without-
coronavirus-patients-see-empty-beds-and-dark-hallways-instead/article_
bf54d7f4-2c17-5aa1-84d8-f6b89c00fa83.html.

11. Kirk Siegler, "Small-Town Hospitals Are Closing Just as Coronavirus
Arrives in Rural America," NPR, April 9, 2020, https://www.npr.
org/2020/04/09/829753752/small-town-hospitals-are-closing-just-as-
coronavirus-arrives-in-rural-america.

12. Ibid.

13. "Child's Lemonade Stand Shut Down for No Permit," NBC-2, May 31,
2018, https://www.nbc-2.com/story/38314612/childs-lemonade-stand-shut-
down-for-no-permit.

14. Jana Randow and Yuko Takeo, "Negative Interest Rates," Bloomberg,
November 1, 2019, https://www.bloomberg.com/quicktake/negative-
interest-rates.

15. Mike Bird, "This Is Why Cash Should Be Illegal," *Business Insider,*
March 25, 2015, https://www.businessinsider.com/why-cash-should-be-
illegal-2015-3.

16. Scott Rodd, "As More California Businesses Go Cashless During
Pandemic, Lawmaker Continues Push to Ban the Practice," Capradio,
May 12, 2020, https://www.capradio.org/articles/2020/05/12/as-more-
california-businesses-go-cashless-during-pandemic-lawmaker-continues-
push-to-ban-the-practice/.

17. Kent Wainscott, "New Normal: Cards over Cash," WISN 12, May
11, 2020, https://www.wisn.com/article/new-normal-cards-over-
cash/32421005#.

18. Bill Gardner, "Dirty Banknotes May Be Spreading the Coronavirus,
WHO Suggests," *Telegraph,* March 2, 2020, https://www.telegraph.co.uk/
news/2020/03/02/exclusive-dirty-banknotes-may-spreading-coronavirus-
world-health/.

19. Meera Jagannathan, "World Health Organization: 'We did NOT say
that cash was transmitting coronavirus,'" MarketWatch, March 9, 2020,

https://www.marketwatch.com/story/who-we-did-not-say-that-cash-was-transmitting-coronavirus-2020-03-06.

20. David D. Kirkpatrick, "$1.2 Billion from U.S. to Drugmaker to Pursue Coronavirus Vaccine," *New York Times,* May 21, 2020, https://www.nytimes.com/2020/05/21/health/coronavirus-vaccine-astrazeneca.html.

21. Kevin Liptak, Jim Acosta, and Kaitlan Collins, "White House Names Heads of 'Warp Speed' Coronavirus Vaccine Effort," CNN, May 13, 2020, https://www.cnn.com/2020/05/13/politics/white-house-coronavirus-vaccine/index.html.

22. Kevin Liptak, Kaitlan Collins, and Jeremy Diamond, "Trump's New Vaccine Chief Will Donate Stock Windfall to Cancer Research," CNN, May 18, 2020, https://edition.cnn.com/2020/05/18/politics/moncef-slaoui-moderna-stocks-coronavirus-vaccine/index.html.

23. Denise Grady, "Moderna Coronavirus Vaccine Trial Shows Promising Early Results," *New York Times,* May 18, 2020, https://www.nytimes.com/2020/05/18/health/coronavirus-vaccine-moderna.html.

24. Liptak, Collins, and Diamond, "Trump's New Vaccine Chief Will Donate Stock Windfall to Cancer Research."

25. Rachel Sharp, "REVEALED: Two executives at drug firm Moderna quietly sold nearly $30 million of stock when they unveiled coronavirus vaccine and value rose—before share price went down again," *Daily Mail,* May 23, 2020, https://www.dailymail.co.uk/news/article-8350419/Moderna-executives-offloaded-nearly-30-million-stocks-day-unveiling-coronavirus-vaccine.html.

26. Christopher Rowland, "Taxpayers Paid to Develop Remdesivir but Will Have No Say When Gilead Sets Price," *Houston Chronicle*, May 26, 2020, https://www.chron.com/business/article/Taxpayers-paid-to-develop-remdesivir-but-will-15296173.php.

27. "Report: 7.5M Small Businesses at Risk of Closing as Result of Coronavirus Pandemic," CBS2/KCAL9, April 29, 2020, https://losangeles.cbslocal.com/2020/04/29/coronavirus-small-businesses-closing/.

28. Executive Order No. 2020-91 Safeguards to protect Michigan's workers from COVID-19, State of Michigan Office of the Governor, May 18, 2020, https://content.govdelivery.com/attachments/MIEOG/2020/05/18/file_attachments/1453892/EO%202020-91.pdf.

29. Ibid.

30. Jessica Silver-Greenberg, David Enrich, Jesse Drucker, and Stacy Cowley, "Large, Troubled Companies Got Bailout Money in Small-Business Loan Program," *New York Times,* April 26, 2020 (updated May 13, 2020),

https://www.nytimes.com/2020/04/26/business/coronavirus-small-business-loans-large-companies.html.

31. "Hospitals Got Bailouts and Furloughed Thousands While Paying C.E.O.s Millions," DNYUZ, June 8, 2020, https://dnyuz.com/2020/06/08/hospitals-got-bailouts-and-furloughed-thousands-while-paying-c-e-o-s-millions/.

32. Ibid.

33. Jesse Drucker, Jessica Silver-Greenberg, and Sarah Kliff, "Wealthiest Hospitals Got Billions in Bailout for Struggling Health Providers," *New York Times,* May 25, 2020, https://www.nytimes.com/2020/05/25/business/coronavirus-hospitals-bailout.html.

34. Lachlan Markay, Sam Brodey, William Bredderman, and Jackie Kucinich, "Trump's Small Biz Rescue Bailed Out Kushner's Family, Obama's Aides and Other Political Elite." Daily Beast, July 6, 2020, https://www.thedailybeast.com/trumps-small-biz-rescue-bailed-out-kushners-family-obamas-aides-and-other-political-elite.

35. Ibid.

36. Christopher Rugaber, "Kanye West? The Girl Scouts? Hedge funds? All got PPP loans," Associated Press, July 6, 2020, https://apnews.com/8798e58a0ddc490ad549329b343e551c.

37. Jessica Bursztynsky, "Here are some of the tech start-ups that took government payroll loans during the coronavirus crisis." CNBC, July 6, 2020, https://www.cnbc.com/2020/07/06/ppp-loans-to-tech-start-ups-bird-mixpanel-grindr-on-the-list.html.

38. "$30 BILLION in "Paycheck Protection" loans went to companies reporting ZERO jobs retained," MichaelSavage.com, July 7, 2020, https://michaelsavage.com/30-billion-in-paycheck-protection-loans-went-to-companies-reporting-zero-jobs-retained/.

39. Danielle Kurtzleben, "Small Businesses Say Rescue Loans Come with Too Many Strings Attached," NPR, April 28, 2020, https://www.npr.org/2020/04/28/845930096/small-businesses-say-rescue-loans-come-with-too-many-strings-attached.

CHAPTER 3: WILL OUR BOLD PEASANTRY GO GENTLY INTO THAT GOOD NIGHT?

1. Oliver Goldsmith, "The Deserted Village," Poetry Foundation, https://www.poetryfoundation.org/poems/44292/the-deserted-village.

2. "Man Detained Outside of Restaurant Defying Fresno's Stay-at-Home Order," Fox 26 News, May 10, 2020, https://kmph.com/news/local/man-arrested-outside-of-restaurant-defying-fresnos-stay-at-home-order.

3. David Yaffe-Bellany and Michael Corkery, "Dumped Milk, Smashed Eggs, Plowed Vegetables: Food Waste of the Pandemic," *New York Times,* April 11, 2020, https://www.nytimes.com/2020/04/11/business/coronavirus-destroying-food.html?auth=login-email&login=email.

4. Dominique Patton, "China to Auction 10,000 Tonnes of Pork from Reserves on April 16—Notice," Reuters, April 14, 2020, https://www.reuters.com/article/china-pork-reserves/china-to-auction-10000-tonnes-of-pork-from-reserves-on-april-16-notice-idUSP8N2BU01Q.

5. Anjali Fluker, "Coronavirus: Largest U.S. Restaurant Firm Outlines Emergency Pay for Workers & More," *Orlando Business Journal,* March 19, 2020, https://www.bizjournals.com/orlando/news/2020/03/19/coronaviruslargest-u-s-restaurant-firm-outlines.html.

6. Thomas Franck, "US Grocery Costs Jump the Most in 46 Years, Led by Rising Prices for Meat and Eggs," CNBC, May 12, 2020, https://www.cnbc.com/2020/05/12/us-grocery-costs-jump-the-most-in-46-years-led-by-rising-prices-for-meat-and-eggs.html.

7. Lauren Edwards, "Beloved Music Store Closing in Hastings, Heartbroken Owner Says 'This Is My Dream,'" Fox 17, March 4, 2020, https://www.fox17online.com/news/coronavirus/beloved-music-store-closing-in-hastings-heartbroken-owner-says-this-is-my-dream.

8. Ron Hilliard, "Owosso Barber Defies Governor's order, Reopens Shop," Fox 25, May 4, 2020, https://nbc25news.com/news/coronavirus/owosso-barber-defies-governor-order-and-opens-back-up-for-business.

9. Ed White, "Michigan strikes back by suspending license of elderly barber who cut hair despite order to stay closed," ABC News, May 13, 2020, https://abc7news.com/health/state-suspends-elderly-barbers-license-after-he-defied-closure-order/6179571/.

10. Hilliard, "Owosso Barber Defies Governor's order, Reopens Shop."

11. Moriah Balingit, "Armed militia helped a Michigan barbershop open, a coronavirus defiance that puts Republican lawmakers in a bind," *Washington Post,* May 12, 2020, https://www.washingtonpost.com/national/coronavirus-michigan-republicans-whitmer/2020/05/12/54975e1a-9466-11ea-82b4-c8db161ff6e5_story.html.

12. "Whitmer: Protests at Capitol 'Make It Likelier' Stay-at-Home Will Be Extended," WXYZ Detroit, May 13, 2020, https://www.wxyz.com/news/coronavirus/whitmer-protests-at-capitol-make-it-likelier-stay-at-home-will-be-extended.

13. "Michigan Governor Says 'Some of the Worst Racism' Fueled Protests over Coronavirus Response," CBS News, May 4, 2020, https://www.cbsnews.com/news/michigan-protests-racism-governor-whitmer/.

14. Stephen Sorace, "Washington police officer on leave after video post about not enforcing 'tyrannical' coronavirus measures," Fox News, May 13, 2020, https://www.foxnews.com/us/washington-police-officer-video-coronavirus-measures.

15. Greg Anderson, "Greg Anderson: Officers doing the right thing?," YouTube, May 7, 2020, https://www.youtube.com/watch?v=b29gsJ3ZAQ4.

16. Erica Werner, "House Democrats Pass $3 Trillion Coronavirus Relief Bill Despite Trump's Veto Threat," *Washington Post*, May 15, 2020, https://www.washingtonpost.com/us-policy/2020/05/15/democrats-pelosi-congress-coronavirus-3-trillion-trump/.

17. Gilbert Magallon, "Business Owners Say Employees Are Reluctant to Come Back to Work," ABC 30 Action News, May 15, 2020, https://abc30.com/business/business-owners-say-employees-are-reluctant-to-come-back-to-work/6184250/.

18. Nicole Narea, "The House's Latest Coronavirus Relief Bill Gives Stimulus Payments to Unauthorized Immigrants," *Vox*, May 16, 2020, https://www.vox.com/2020/5/16/21260906/house-stimulus-check-immigrants-heroes-act.

19. "Sacrificing for the Common Good: Rationing in WWII," National Park Service, https://www.nps.gov/articles/rationing-in-wwii.htm.

20. Noah Higgins-Dunn and Kevin Breuninger, "Cuomo Says It's 'Shocking' Most New Coronavirus Hospitalizations Are People Who Had Been Staying Home," CNBC, May 6, 2020, https://www.cnbc.com/2020/05/06/ny-gov-cuomo-says-its-shocking-most-new-coronavirus-hospitalizations-are-people-staying-home.html.

CHAPTER 4: HIJACKING MARTIN LUTHER KING'S DREAM

1. Danielle Wallace and Travis Fedschun, "Australian Officials Charged Nearly 200 with Fire Offenses as Deadly Wildfires Rage," Fox News, January 7, 2020, https://www.foxnews.com/world/australia-brush-fire-24-charged-new-south-wales.

2. Bettina Boxall, "Human-Caused Ignitions Spark California's Worst Wildfires but Get Little State Focus," *Los Angeles Times,* January 5, 2020, https://www.latimes.com/environment/story/2020-01-05/human-caused-ignitions-spark-california-worst-wildfires.

3. Hinnerk Feldwisch-Drentrup, "How WHO Became China's Coronavirus Accomplice," *Foreign Policy,* April 2, 2020, https://foreignpolicy.com/2020/04/02/china-coronavirus-who-health-soft-power/.

4. John R. Lott Jr., "Liberal Politicians Who Order Police to Stand Down Are the Same People Who Want to Ban Guns," *Washington Times,* June

3, 2020, https://www.washingtontimes.com/news/2020/jun/3/liberal-politicians-who-order-police-to-stand-down/.

5. "Honoring Officers Killed in 2020," Officer Down Memorial Page, https://www.odmp.org/search/year/2020.

6. Kathryn Watson, "Trump Says U.S. 'Terminating' Relationship with World Health Organization," CBS News, May 29, 2020, https://www.cbsnews.com/news/trump-united-states-terminating-relationship-world-health-organization/.

7. Arica L. Coleman, "A Riot Started in Newark 50 Years Ago. It Shouldn't Have Been a Surprise," *Time,* July 12, 2017, https://time.com/4854023/newark-riot-1967-lessons/.

8. https://twitter.com/ASavageNation/status/1266049598755233792?s=20.

9. Marcus Tullius Cicero, *De Officiis*, Book II. Loeb Classical Library, 1913, p. 250, https://penelope.uchicago.edu/Thayer/E/Roman/Texts/Cicero/de_Officiis/2B*.html.

10. Jacob Ward, "George Floyd Death and Minneapolis Protests," NBC News, May 30, 2020, https://www.nbcnews.com/news/us-news/live-blog/george-floyd-death-minneapolis-protests-live-updates-n1217886.

11. Tal Axelrod, "St. Paul Mayor Says Arrested Protesters Were from out of State," *Hill,* May 30, 2020, https://thehill.com/homenews/state-watch/500268-st-paul-mayor-says-arrested-protesters-were-from-out-of-state.

12. Sergei Klebnikov and Rachel Sander, "Mayor Walks Back Statement Saying Every Person Arrested in Minneapolis Protests Was from out of State," *Forbes,* May 30, 2020, https://www.forbes.com/sites/sergeiklebnikov/2020/05/30/mayor-says-he-was-incorrect-in-saying-every-person-arrested-in-minneapolis-protests-was-from-out-of-state/#7870ec00233c.

13. Michael Savage, *Stop Mass Hysteria: America's Insanity From the Salem Witch Trials to the Trump Witch Hunt, From the Red Scare to Russian Collusion* (New York: Hachette, 2018), 1.

14. Ibid., 5.

15. "Thomas Jefferson to John Norvell, June 11, 1807," Library of Congress, https://www.loc.gov/resource/mtj1.038_0592_0594/?sp=2&st=text.

16. Dan Lamothe, Missy Ryan, Paul Sonne, and Josh Dawsey, "Pentagon Chief Balks at Trump's Call for Active-Duty Military Force on U.S. Citizens, and Mattis Rips President," *Washington Post,* June 3, 2020, https://www.washingtonpost.com/national-security/despite-suggestions-from-trump-pentagon-chief-says-he-does-not-support-invoking-insurrection-act/2020/06/03/8e8dad2e-a59e-11ea-8681-7d471bf20207_story.html.

17. Jeffrey Goldberg, "James Mattis Denounces President Trump, Describes Him as a Threat to the Constitution," *Atlantic,* June 3, 2020, https://www.theatlantic.com/politics/archive/2020/06/james-mattis-denounces-trump-protests-militarization/612640/.

18. Charles M. Blow, "Let's Rescue the Race Debate," *New York Times,* November 19, 2010, https://www.nytimes.com/2010/11/20/opinion/20blow.html.

19. Martin Luther King Jr. "I Have a Dream" speech, National Archives, https://www.archives.gov/files/press/exhibits/dream-speech.pdf.

20. Althea Legaspi, "Watch Oprah's 'Where Do We Go from Here?' Special with Black Thought Leaders," *Rolling Stone,* June 10, 2020, https://www.rollingstone.com/tv/tv-news/oprah-where-do-we-go-from-here-special-watch-1013385/.

21. https://twitter.com/ASavageNation/status/1270762594240876544?s=20.

22. Cuneyt Dil, "African American Reparation Bill Passes California Assembly," KCRA, June 11, 2020, https://www.kcra.com/article/african-american-reparation-bill-passes-california-assembly/32843430.

23. Jeffery Martin, "Joe Biden Wants to See Studies About Feasibility of Slavery Reparations," *Newsweek,* June 10, 2020, https://www.newsweek.com/joe-biden-wants-see-studies-about-feasibility-slavery-reparations-1510096.

24. Feliks Garcia, "Women's March: Madonna Said She Thought about 'Blowing Up White House' but 'Chose Love' Instead," *Independent,* January 21, 2017, https://www.independent.co.uk/news/world/americas/madonna-blow-up-white-house-womens-march-washington-donald-trump-president-protest-latest-a7539741.html.

25. Dan Alexander, "How Barack Obama Has Made $20 Million Since Arriving in Washington," *Forbes,* January 20, 2017, https://www.forbes.com/sites/danalexander/2017/01/20/how-barack-obama-has-made-20-million-since-arriving-in-washington/#4bbddaac5bf0.

26. Katie Reilly, "Read President Obama's Speech from the Dallas Memorial Service," *Time,* July 12, 2016, https://time.com/4403543/president-obama-dallas-shooting-memorial-service-speech-transcript/.

27. Heather Mac Donald, "The Myth of Systemic Police Racism," *Wall Street Journal,* June 2, 2020, https://www.wsj.com/articles/the-myth-of-systemic-police-racism-11591119883.

28. Ibid.

29. Ibid.

30. Margaret Abrams, "Who Is David Geffen? The Man Vacationing with Oprah, Katy Perry, Jeff Bezos and Lauren Sanchez on His Yacht *Rising*

Sun," *ES Insider,* August 7, 2019, https://www.standard.co.uk/insider/alist/who-is-david-geffen-meet-the-man-vacationing-with-oprah-katy-perry-jeff-bezos-and-lauren-sanchez-on-a4207136.html.

31. Alexander Bolton, "Harris Grapples with Defund the Police Movement amid Veep Talk," June 11, 2020, https://thehill.com/homenews/campaign/502187-harris-grapples-with-defund-the-police-movement-amid-veep-talk.

32. Kenneth Shores and Simon Ejdemyr, "Do School Districts Spend Less Money on Poor and Minority Students?," Brookings, May 25, 2017, https://www.brookings.edu/blog/brown-center-chalkboard/2017/05/25/do-school-districts-spend-less-money-on-poor-and-minority-students/.

33. "New Poll: 80 Percent Want to Keep, Increase Police Funding," *Newsmax,* June 9, 2020, https://www.newsmax.com/us/police-funding-national-sheriffs/2020/06/09/id/971415/.

34. "Most Reject Calls for Defunding Police," Rasmussen Reports, June 9, 2020, https://www.rasmussenreports.com/public_content/politics/current_events/social_issues/most_reject_calls_for_defunding_police.

35. Cristina Marcos, "Pelosi, Schumer Kneel in Silence for Almost 9 Minutes to Honor George Floyd," *Hill,* June 8, 2020, https://thehill.com/homenews/house/501633-pelosi-schumer-kneel-in-silence-for-almost-9-minutes-to-honor-george-floyd.

36. https://twitter.com/obianuju/status/1270053042340139008?s=20.

37. Nana Efua Mumford, "Democratic Leaders' Kneeling Was Fine. The Kente Cloth Was Not," *Washington Post,* June 11, 2020, https://www.washingtonpost.com/opinions/2020/06/11/educate-yourself-before-you-wear-kente/.

38. "Nancy Pelosi: I'm Kneeling and I Can't Get Up," Shore News Network, June 9, 2020, http://www.shorenewsnetwork.com/2020/06/09/nancy-pelosi-i-cant-get-up/.

39. "Nadler Did Not Kneel," CNS News, June 8, 2020, https://www.cnsnews.com/blog/cnsnewscom-staff/nadler-did-not-kneel.

CHAPTER 5: A PUBLIC HEALTH DISASTER

1. Feijun Luo, PhD, corresponding author Curtis S. Florence, PhD, Myriam Quispe-Agnoli, PhD, Lijing Ouyang, PhD, and Alexander E. Crosby, MD, "Impact of Business Cycles on US Suicide Rates, 1928–2007," *American Journal of Public Health* 101, no. 6 (June 2011): 1139–46, https://www.ncbi.nlm.nih.gov/pmc/articles/PMC3093269/.

2. Jennifer Smith, "Cuomo admits his decision to quarantine everyone at once was 'not the best strategy' and that he is 'working on' release of coronavirus antibody test that will allow people to go back to work," *Daily*

Mail, March 26, 2020, https://www.dailymail.co.uk/news/article-8156457/
Cuomo-says-probably-not-best-strategy-quarantine-once.html.

3. Alison Bateman-House, MA, MPH, and Amy Fairchild, PhD, MPH,
   "Medical Examination of Immigrants at Ellis Island," *American Medical
   Association Journal of Ethics* 10, no. 4 (April 2008): 235–41.

4. Ibid.

5. Allison Aubrey, "Trump Declares Coronavirus a Public Health Emergency
   and Restricts Travel From China," NPR, January 31, 2020, https://www.
   npr.org/sections/health-shots/2020/01/31/801686524/trump-declares-
   coronavirus-a-public-health-emergency-and-restricts-travel-from-c.

6. Rick Gladstone, "Coronavirus Outbreak Risks Reviving Stigma for
   China," *New York Times,* February 10, 2020, https://www.nytimes.
   com/2020/02/10/world/asia/china-epidemics-coronavirus.html.

7. Catherine E. Shoichet, "The US Coronavirus Travel Ban Could Backfire.
   Here's How," CNN, February 7, 2020, https://www.cnn.com/2020/02/07/
   health/coronavirus-travel-ban/index.html.

8. Ibid.

9. Ashley Parker, Yasmeen Abutaleb, and Lena H. Sun, "Squandered
   Time: How the Trump Administration Lost Control of the
   Coronavirus," *Washington Post*, March 7, 2020, https://www.
   washingtonpost.com/politics/trump-coronavirus-response-squandered-
   time/2020/03/07/5c47d3d0-5fcb-11ea-9055-5fa12981bbbf_story.html.

10. Ibid.

11. Tal Axelrod, "Beijing Criticizes Trump Order Barring Foreign Nationals
    Who Visited China amid Outbreak," *Hill*, February 1, 2020, https://thehill.
    com/policy/international/asia-pacific/481016-beijing-criticizes-trump-
    order-barring-foreign-nationals.

12. Thomas Lifson. "Illegal immigrant flood bringing disease outbreaks,"
    American Thinker, June 8, 2014, http://www.americanthinker.com.
    s3-website-us-east-1.amazonaws.com/blog/2014/06/illegal_immigrant_
    flood_bringing_disease_outbreaks.html.

13. Max Fisher, "How Worried Should You Be About the Coronavirus?" *New
    York Times*, March 6, 2020, https://www.nytimes.com/2020/03/05/world/
    coronavirus-interpreter.html.

14. Denise Grady, "How Does the Coronavirus Compare with the Flu?," *New
    York Times,* March 6, 2020, https://www.nytimes.com/2020/02/29/health/
    coronavirus-flu.html.

15. Sarah Chodosh, "These Charts Show Who Is Most Vulnerable to COVID-
    19," *Popular Science*, March 5, 2020, https://www.popsci.com/story/
    health/covid-19-coronavirus-death-rate-by-age/.

16. Morbidity and Mortality Weekly Report (MMWR), Centers for Disease Control and Prevention, https://www.cdc.gov/mmwr/index.html.

17. Eva Emerson, "Researcher Teases Out Secrets from Surprisingly 'Intelligent' Viruses," *USC News,* October 30, 1998, https://news.usc.edu/9791/researcher-teases-out-secrets-from-surprisingly-intelligent-viruses/.

18. Steven Mosher, "Don't Buy China's Story: The Coronavirus May Have Leaked from a Lab," *New York Post,* February 22, 2020, https://nypost.com/2020/02/22/dont-buy-chinas-story-the-coronavirus-may-have-leaked-from-a-lab/?utm_source=twitter_sitebuttons&utm_medium=site%20buttons&utm_campaign=site%20buttons.

19. Ibid.

20. "Positive RT-PCR Test Results in Patients Recovered From COVID-19," *Journal of the American Medical Association (JAMA),* February 27, 2020, https://jamanetwork.com/journals/jama/fullarticle/2762452.

21. Ibid.

22. Newsmax TV, https://twitter.com/newsmax/status/1246131288664408064?s=20.

23. https://twitter.com/ASavageNation/status/1219679957368000512?s=20.

24. https://twitter.com/ASavageNation/status/1220378258102833153?s=20.

25. Patrick Howley, "EXCLUSIVE: Deborah Birx's Medical License Is Expired," National File, April 4, 2020, https://nationalfile.com/exclusive-deborah-birxs-medical-license-is-expired/.

26. Jayne O'Donnell, "Top Disease Official: Risk of Coronavirus in USA Is 'Minuscule'; Skip Mask and Wash Hands," *USA Today,* February 17, 2020, https://www.usatoday.com/story/news/health/2020/02/17/nih-disease-official-anthony-fauci-risk-of-coronavirus-in-u-s-is-minuscule-skip-mask-and-wash-hands/4787209002/.

27. Veronica Stracqualursi, "Fauci Says He Wears a Mask to Be a Symbol of What 'You Should Be Doing,'" CNN, May 27, 2020, https://www.cnn.com/2020/05/27/politics/fauci-coronavirus-wear-masks-cnntv/index.html.

28. Berkeley Lovelace Jr., "Dr. Anthony Fauci Warns Senators of 'Suffering and Death' if States Reopen Too Early," CNBC, May 12, 2020, https://www.cnbc.com/2020/05/12/dr-anthony-fauci-warns-senators-of-suffering-and-death-if-states-reopen-too-early.html.

29. Berkeley Lovelace Jr., "Dr. Anthony Fauci Says Staying Closed for Too Long Could Cause 'Irreparable Damage,'" CNBC, May 22, 2020, https://www.cnbc.com/2020/05/22/dr-anthony-fauci-says-staying-closed-for-too-long-could-cause-irreparable-damage.html.

30. Ibid.

31. Devan Cole, "Fauci Admits Earlier Covid-19 Mitigation Efforts Would Have Saved More American Lives," CNN, April 12, 2020, https://www.cnn.com/2020/04/12/politics/anthony-fauci-pushback-coronavirus-measures-cnntv/index.html.

32. https://twitter.com/realDonaldTrump/status/1249470237726081030?s=20.

33. https://twitter.com/realDonaldTrump/status/1274006223013249026?s=20.

34. Monica Alba, Carol E. Lee, and Kristen Welker, "Top Members of Coronavirus Task Force Advised Against Trump's Tulsa Rally," NBC News, June 19, 2020, https://www.nbcnews.com/politics/2020-election/top-members-coronavirus-task-force-advised-against-trump-s-tulsa-n1231585.

CHAPTER 6: BEWARE THE TRUE BELIEVERS

1. NBC Bay Area Staff, "Nancy Pelosi Visits San Francisco's Chinatown Amid Coronavirus Concerns," NBC Bay Area, February 24, 2020, https://www.nbcbayarea.com/news/local/nancy-pelosi-visits-san-franciscos-chinatown/2240247/.

2. Ben Lowsen, "Did Xi Jinping Deliberately Sicken the World?," *Diplomat,* April 15, 2020, https://thediplomat.com/2020/04/did-xi-jinping-deliberately-sicken-the-world/.

3. Thomas Jefferson. "From Thomas Jefferson to Peter Carr, with Enclosure, 10 August 1787," National Archives, https://founders.archives.gov/documents/Jefferson/01-12-02-0021.

CHAPTER 7: THE WAR ON OUR LIBERTY

1. David Ingram, "San Francisco Orders Public Not to Leave Home 'Except for Essential Needs,'" NBC News, March 16, 2020, https://www.nbcnews.com/health/health-news/san-francisco-require-people-stay-home-except-essential-needs-n1160916.

2. Dennis Normile, "Coronavirus Cases Have Dropped Sharply in South Korea. What's the Secret to Its Success?," *Science*, March 17, 2020, https://www.sciencemag.org/news/2020/03/coronavirus-cases-have-dropped-sharply-south-korea-whats-secret-its-success.

3. "Mayoral Proclamation of a State of Emergency Due to Covid-19," Civil District Court for the Parish of New Orleans. State of Louisiana Division F, Docket 7, March 11, 2020, http://www.nola.gov/mayor/executive-orders/emergency-declarations/20200311-mayoral-proclamation-of-a-state-of-emergency-due-to-covid-19/.

4. Chris Eger, "2A Group Warns New Orleans over Limiting Gun Sales, Transport," Guns.com, March 17, 2020, https://www.guns.com/

news/2020/03/17/2a-group-warns-new-orleans-over-limiting-gun-sales-transport.

5. Kate Pavlich, "Banning the Sale of Firearms and Ammunition Because of Wuhan Virus? An Illinois Mayor Just Signed an Executive Order to Do It," *Town Hall*, March 13, 2020, https://townhall.com/tipsheet/katiepavlich/2020/03/13/illinois-mayor-may-ban-firearms-ammunition-as-part-of-emergency-over-wuhan-virus-n2564916.

6. Liam Ford, "Mayor of Champaign Declares Emergency over Coronavirus, but City Assures It's Not Banning Gun, Alcohol Sales or Seizing Property," *Chicago Tribune*, March 14, 2020, https://www.chicagotribune.com/coronavirus/ct-coronavirus-champaign-emergency-guns-alcohol-sales-20200314-x36zrgm5pfhf5a4z5q22bjiv6q-story.html.

7. Terence P. Jeffery, "Yes, Virginia's Governor Has Made It a Crime for More Than 10 People to Attend a Church Service," *CNS News*, March 25, 2020, https://www.cnsnews.com/commentary/terence-p-jeffrey/yes-virginias-governor-has-made-it-crime-more-10-people-attend-church.

8. "§ 44-146.17. Powers and duties of Governor," Code of Virginia, https://law.lis.virginia.gov/vacode/title44/chapter3.2/section44-146.17/.

9. Constitution of Virginia, Article I, Section 16, https://law.lis.virginia.gov/constitution/article1/section16/.

10. NYS Executive Law Article 2-B, http://www.dhses.ny.gov/laws-policies/documents/Exec-Law-Art-2B-2018.pdf.

11. Ron Brackett and Jan Wesner Childs, "Coronavirus Updates: 15 States Have Stay at Home Orders; 'This Week, It's Going to Get Bad,' U.S. Surgeon General Says," Weather Channel, March 23, 2020, https://weather.com/health/coronavirus/news/2020-03-23-coronavirus-updates-number-of-cases-lockdowns-quarantines-united.

12. https://www.merriam-webster.com/dictionary/liberal#h1.

13. Tim Hains, "Bill de Blasio Suggests 'Nationalization of Crucial Factories and Industries That Produce Medical Supplies,'" *Real Clear Politics*, March 15, 2020, https://www.realclearpolitics.com/video/2020/03/15/bill_de_blasio_suggests_nationalization_of_crucial_factories_and_industries_that_could_produce_the_medical_supplies.html.

14. Eddy Rodriguez, "Actor Sean Penn Says in Op-ed That U.S. Military Should Intervene in Coronavirus Fight," *Newsweek,* March 21, 2020, https://www.newsweek.com/actor-sean-penn-says-op-ed-that-us-military-should-intervene-coronavirus-fight-1493573.

15. VideoNation and Brett Story, "Sean Penn Reflects on the Realities of Chavez and Castro," *Nation*, November 25, 2008, https://www.thenation.com/article/archive/sean-penn-reflects-realities-chavez-and-castro/.

16. Benjamin Lee and Scott Bixby, "Sean Penn on El Chapo Interview: 'I Have a Terrible Regret,'" *Guardian*, January 15, 2016, https://www.theguardian.com/film/2016/jan/15/sean-penn-on-el-chapo-interview-i-have-a-terrible-regret.

17. https://twitter.com/ASavageNation/status/1240058570080542720?s=20.

18. Justin Caruso, "Homeless People in San Francisco Hotel Rooms Are Being Given Free Alcohol and Drugs," *Daily Caller*, May 6, 2020, https://dailycaller.com/2020/05/06/homeless-people-san-francisco-hotel-rooms-given-free-alcohol-and-drugs/.

19. SFDPH Twitter account, May 6, 2020, https://twitter.com/SF_DPH/status/1257546134135861254.

20. Michael Savage, "Homeless Bring Diseases to Cities—Time to Remove Them from Streets," *Newsmax,* February 21, 2018, https://www.newsmax.com/michaelsavage/homeless-san-francisco-rotavirus/2018/02/21/id/844645/.

21. "NYC Looks to Release 1,000+ Inmates as Tri-State Jails Try to Manage COVID-19 Spread," NBC New York, March 23, 2020, https://www.nbcnewyork.com/news/local/jails-in-crisis-tri-state-prisoners-slowly-released-to-manage-covid-19-spread/2339878/.

22. James Turpin, "Sen. Kamala Harris Wants Release of Federal Prison Inmates Considered COVID-19 At-Risk," Fox26 News, March 25, 2020, https://kmph.com/news/local/sen-kamala-harris-wants-inmates-considered-at-risk-for-covis-19-released-from-prison.

23. David Aaro, "US Starts to Release Inmates Due to Coronavirus Outbreak," Fox News, March 20, 2020, https://www.foxnews.com/health/us-starts-release-inmates-coronavirus.

24. Jonah Walters, "Empty the Jails Now," *Jacobin*, March 24, 2020, https://www.jacobinmag.com/2020/03/prison-jail-coronavirus-release-abolition-incarceration.

25. Victoria Taft, "Peak Buffoonery: Paddleboarder in Ocean Off Malibu Is Arrested for Not Socially Distancing," PJ Media, April 3, 2020, https://pjmedia.com/lifestyle/peak-buffoonery-paddleboarder-in-ocean-off-malibu-is-arrested-for-not-socially-distancing/.

26. Richard W. Lieban, "Sorcery, Illness and Social Control in a Philippine Municipality," *Southwestern Journal of Anthropology* 16, no. 2 (Summer 1960).

27. Lauren Edmonds, "Shocking moment a police officer bodyslams a woman in an Alabama Walmart 'for refusing to wear a face mask' amid the coronavirus pandemic," *Daily Mail,* May 7, 2020, https://www.dailymail.co.uk/news/article-8297667/Police-officer-

bodyslams-woman-Alabama-Walmart-refusing-wear-face-mask.
html?ico=embedded.

28. Kim Bellware, "Violent Arrest in New York Raises Questions about
Police Enforcement of Social Distancing Orders," *Washington Post,* May
5, 2020, https://www.washingtonpost.com/nation/2020/05/05/donni-
wright-nyc-arrest/.

CHAPTER 8: THE WAR ON OUR CONSTITUTION

1. Jason Silversteen, "43 States Now Have Stay-at-Home Orders for
Coronavirus. These Are the 7 That Don't," CBS News, April 6, 2020,
https://www.cbsnews.com/news/stay-at-home-orders-states/.

2. Ken Dilanian and Dan De Luce, "Trump Administration's Lack of a
Unified Coronavirus Strategy Will Cost Lives, Say a Dozen Experts,"
NBC News, April 3, 2020, https://www.nbcnews.com/politics/donald-
trump/trump-administration-s-lack-unified-coronavirus-strategy-will-cost-
lives-n1175126.

3. James Madison, "The Alleged Danger From the Powers of the Union to the
State Governments Considered for the Independent Journal," "Federalist
Papers: Primary Documents in American History." Library of Congress.
https://guides.loc.gov/federalist-papers/text-41-50

4. President Donald Trump, "Letter from President Donald J. Trump to
Senator Charles E. Schumer," White House, April 2, 2020, https://www.
whitehouse.gov/briefings-statements/letter-president-donald-j-trump-
senator-charles-e-schumer/.

5. Lia Eustachewich, "New Study Says Summer Sun Can Kill Coronavirus
in 34 Minutes," *New York Post,* June 23, 2020, https://nypost.
com/2020/06/23/new-study-says-summer-sun-can-kill-coronavirus-in-
34-minutes/.

6. Elizabeth Thomas and Jordyn Phelps, "Trump Claims He, Not Governors,
Has Power over States on Deciding Reopening Country," ABC News, April
13, 2020, https://abcnews.go.com/Politics/trump-claims-governors-power-
states-deciding-reopening-country/story?id=70119115.

7. Jane C. Timm and Pete Williams, "Trump Claims It's His Call on When
to 'Reopen' the Country. He's Wrong," NBC News, April 13, 2020, https://
www.nbcnews.com/politics/donald-trump/fact-check-trump-claims-it-s-
his-call-when-reopen-n1182836.

8. Rebecca Shabad, "Cuomo Warns of Constitutional Crisis 'Like You
Haven't Seen in Decades' if Trump Tries to Reopen New York," NBC
News, April 14, 2020, https://www.nbcnews.com/politics/politics-news/
cuomo-says-if-trump-tries-reopen-new-york-then-we-n1183341.

9. "Remarks by President Trump on Vaccine Development," White House, May 15, 2020, https://www.whitehouse.gov/briefings-statements/remarks-president-trump-vaccine-development/.

10. "Vaccine Effectiveness: How Well Do the Flu Vaccines Work?," Centers for Disease Control, https://www.cdc.gov/flu/vaccines-work/vaccineeffect.htm.

11. Ibid.

12. "From SARS to MERS, Thrusting Coronaviruses into the Spotlight," U.S. National Library of Medicine/National Institutes of Health, January 14, 2019, https://www.ncbi.nlm.nih.gov/pmc/articles/PMC6357155/.

13. Amy Graff, "The Most Commonly Stolen Book at the San Francisco Public Library May Surprise You," *SFGate*, February 14, 2020, https://www.sfgate.com/bayarea/article/most-commonly-stolen-book-library-Michael-Savage-15045259.php.

14. Emma Newburger, "Obama Warns Democrats against Going Too Far Left: 'We Have to Be Rooted in Reality,'" CNBC, November 16, 2019, https://www.cnbc.com/2019/11/16/obama-warns-democrats-against-going-too-far-left.html.

15. *Wilson Bulletin* 2, no. 1 (New York: H. W. Wilson, 1922), p. 308.

16. Terisa Estasio, "Call to Action: Feces Complaints Increase in San Francisco," KRON4, November 25, 2019, https://www.kron4.com/news/bay-area/call-to-action-feces-complaints-increase-in-san-francisco/.

17. Adee Braun, "The 19th-Century Night Soil Men Who Carted Away America's Waste," Atlas Obscura, March 15, 2016, https://www.atlasobscura.com/articles/when-american-cities-were-full-of-crap.

18. Megan Fox, "'Model' Assaults #WalkAway Founder Brandon Straka at the Airport for Wearing a MAGA Hat," PJ Media, April 11, 2019, https://pjmedia.com/trending/model-assaults-walkaway-founder-brandon-straka-at-the-airport-for-wearing-a-maga-hat/.

19. John Nolte, "Nolte—Rap Sheet: **389** Media-Approved Hate Crimes Against Trump Supporters," Breitbart, February 20, 2020, https://www.breitbart.com/the-media/2020/02/14/rap-sheet-389-media-approved-hate-crimes-trump-supporters/.

20. Hannah Bleu, "Woman Allegedly Punches Former NYPD Officer over 'Make Fifty Great Again' Hat," February 12, 2020, https://www.breitbart.com/politics/2020/02/12/woman-allegedly-punches-former-nypd-officer-make-fifty-great-again-hat/.

21. Lauren Cross, "'Y'all scared, just like your president': Teen Trump Supporters Run off Road, Police Say," *Northwest Indiana Times,* February 21, 2020, https://www.nwitimes.com/news/local/crime-and-courts/y-all-

scared-just-like-your-president-teen-trump-supporters/article_18ead463-9450-5968-8ef2-91683b2bd6c6.html.

22. Khaleda Rahman, "Pelosi's GOP Challenger Shares Video of Protester Threatening Him in San Francisco: 'I Actually Want You Dead,'" *Newsweek,* February 5, 2020, https://www.newsweek.com/republican-congressional-candidate-claims-threatened-antifa-1485789.

23. Brendan Cole, "Catholic Churches Are Being Desecrated across France—and Officials Don't Know Why," *Newsweek,* March 21, 2019, https://www.newsweek.com/spate-attacks-catholic-churches-france-sees-altars-desecrated-christ-statue-1370800.

24. Egan Millard, "St. John's Church in Washington Vandalized Again," Episcopal News Service, June 23, 2020, https://www.episcopalnewsservice.org/2020/06/23/st-johns-church-in-washington-vandalized-again/.

CHAPTER 9: THE PHONY MODERATE

1. Jordain Carney, "Senate Closes In on Trillion-Dollar Coronavirus Stimulus Bill," *Hill*, March 21, 2020, https://thehill.com/homenews/senate/488782-senate-closes-in-on-trillion-dollar-coronavirus-stimulus-bill.

2. Brandon Waltens, "Stimulus Bill Filled with Wasteful Spending," Texas Scorecard, March 26, 2020, https://texasscorecard.com/federal/stimulus-bill-filled-with-wasteful-spending/.

3. Caitlin Emma, Jennifer Scholtes, and Theodoric Meyer, "Who Got Special Deals in the Stimulus and Why They Got Them," *Politico*, March 26, 2020, https://www.politico.com/news/2020/03/26/stimulus-coronavirus-special-deals-151108.

4. Greg Sargent, "Why Did Trump Win? New Research by Democrats Offers a Worrisome Answer," *Washington Post*, May 1, 2017, https://www.washingtonpost.com/blogs/plum-line/wp/2017/05/01/why-did-trump-win-new-research-by-democrats-offers-a-worrisome-answer/.

5. Martin Pengelly, "Bernie Sanders Says Trump Voters Aren't 'Deplorable' in Jab Aimed at Clinton Camp," *Guardian*, April 1, 2017, https://www.theguardian.com/us-news/2017/apr/01/bernie-sanders-trump-voters-not-deplorable-clinton-warren.

6. David Horsey, "President Sanders? Bernie Would Have Beaten Trump," *Los Angeles Times*, December 22, 2016, https://www.latimes.com/opinion/topoftheticket/la-na-tt-bernie-beats-trump-20161222-story.html.

7. "Polls: Arizona Senate—McSally vs. Kelly," *Real Clear Politics*, March 29, 2020, https://www.realclearpolitics.com/epolls/2020/senate/az/arizona_senate_mcsally_vs_kelly-6801.html.

8. Derek Thompson, "American Migration Patterns Should Terrify the GOP," *Atlantic*, September 17, 2019, https://www.theatlantic.com/ideas/archive/2019/09/american-migration-patterns-should-terrify-gop/598153/.

9. Ibid.

10. Andrew Soergel, "States That Lost Population in 2019," *U.S. News & World Report*, February 4, 2020, https://www.usnews.com/news/best-states/slideshows/us-states-that-lost-population-in-2019?slide=13.

11. Amy Lieu, "4 States Had More Deaths than Births between 2018 and 2019, US Census Shows," Fox2 Detroit, January 1, 2020, https://www.fox2detroit.com/news/4-states-had-more-deaths-than-births-between-2018-and-2019-us-census-shows.

12. "Bernie Sanders on the Issues," Berniesanders.com, April 1, 2020, https://berniesanders.com/issues/.

13. Green New Deal FAQ Fact Sheet, originally published February 7, 2019, republished by the Heartland Institute, https://www.heartland.org/publications-resources/publications/green-new-deal-fact-sheet-and-faq-from-rep-alexandria-ocasio-cortez-and-sen-edward-markey.

14. Pippa Stevens, "US Leads Greenhouse Gas Emissions on a Per Capita Basis, Report Finds," CNBC, November 26, 2019, https://www.cnbc.com/2019/11/26/us-leads-greenhouse-gas-emissions-on-a-per-capita-basis-report-finds.html.

15. Jerri Ann Henry, "We Can Save the Planet Without Destroying the Economy," InsideSources, February 18, 2020, https://www.insidesources.com/we-can-save-the-planet-without-destroying-the-economy/.

16. Ibid.

17. David Harsanyi, "The 10 Most Insane Requirements of the Green New Deal," *Federalist,* February 7, 2019, https://thefederalist.com/2019/02/07/ten-most-insane-requirements-green-new-deal/.

18. Ibid.

19. "Climate: Joe's Plan for a Clean Energy Revolution and Environmental Justice," Biden official campaign website, March 30, 2020, https://joebiden.com/climate/.

20. "College for All," Bernie Sanders official campaign website, https://berniesanders.com/issues/.

21. "Joe's Agenda for Students," Biden official campaign website, March 30, 2020, https://joebiden.com/joes-agenda-for-students/.

22. PK, "Household Income Percentile Calculator for the United States [2019]," DQYDJ, https://dqydj.com/household-income-percentile-calculator/.

23. Jessica Semega, Melissa Kollar, John Creamer, and Abinash Mohanty, "Income and Poverty in the United States: 2018," U.S. Census Bureau, September 2019, https://www.census.gov/content/dam/Census/library/publications/2019/demo/p60-266.pdf.

24. "The Biden Plan to Protect and Build on the Affordable Care Act," Biden official campaign website, March 30, 2020, https://joebiden.com/healthcare/.

25. "Budget Basics: Medicare," Peter G. Peterson Foundation, April 30, 2019, https://www.pgpf.org/budget-basics/medicare.

26. Chris Cilliza, "Andrew Cuomo Said He'll Never Run for President. That's a Mistake," CNN, March 31, 2020, https://www.cnn.com/2020/03/31/politics/andrew-cuomo-2024-2028-president/index.html.

CHAPTER 10: FROM LAW AND ORDER TO RAW DISORDER

1. "Order Regarding Handling and Disposition of Information," United States Foreign Intelligence Surveillance Court, January 7, 2020, http://cdn.cnn.com/cnn/2020/images/01/23/fisc.declassifed.order.16-1182.17-52.17-375.17-679..200123.pdf.

2. Sean Davis, "BREAKING: Spy Court Admits FISA Warrants Against Carter Page Were 'Not Valid," *Federalist*, January 23, 2020, https://thefederalist.com/2020/01/23/breaking-spy-court-admits-fisa-warrants-against-carter-page-were-not-valid/.

3. Jack Shafer, "The Spies Who Came in to the TV Studio," *Politico*, February 6, 2018, https://www.politico.com/magazine/story/2018/02/06/john-brennan-james-claper-michael-hayden-former-cia-media-216943.

4. Sharon LaFraniere and Katie Benner, "Mueller Delivers Report on Trump-Russia Investigation to Attorney General," *New York Times*, March 22, 2019, https://www.nytimes.com/2019/03/22/us/politics/mueller-report.html.

5. Mairead McArdle, "Mueller Resigns, Special Counsel's Office Closes," *National Review*, May 29, 2019, https://www.nationalreview.com/news/mueller-resigns-special-counsels-office-closes/.

6. Eugene Kiely, Lori Robertson, and D'Angelo Gore, "The Whistleblower Complaint Timeline," FactCheck.org, September 27, 2019, https://www.factcheck.org/2019/09/the-whistleblower-complaint-timeline/.

7. Adam Goldman and Michael S. Schmidt, "Rod Rosenstein Suggested Secretly Recording Trump and Discussed 25th Amendment," *New York Times*, September 21, 2018, https://www.nytimes.com/2018/09/21/us/politics/rod-rosenstein-wear-wire-25th-amendment.html.

8. Ronn Blitzer, "Comey Admits 'I Was Wrong' on FISA Conduct, Remains Defiant on Dossier in Tense Interview," Fox News, December 15, 2019,

https://www.foxnews.com/politics/comey-defends-fbis-fisa-process-after-scathing-ig-report.

9. Seumas Milne, "It's Not Russia That's Pushed Ukraine to the Brink of War," *Guardian*, April 30, 2014, https://www.theguardian.com/commentisfree/2014/apr/30/russia-ukraine-war-kiev-conflict.

10. "Ukraine Crisis: Transcript of Leaked Nuland-Pyatt call," BBC, February 7, 2014, https://www.bbc.com/news/world-europe-26079957.

11. Ilya Zhegulev, "Ukraine Widens Probe against Burisma Founder to Embezzlement of State Funds," Reuters, November 20, 2019, https://www.reuters.com/article/us-usa-trump-impeachment-burisma/ukraine-widens-probe-against-burisma-founder-to-embezzlement-of-state-funds-idUSKBN1XU2N7.

12. "Telephone Conversation with President Zelensky of Ukraine," White House, July 25, 2019, https://www.whitehouse.gov/wp-content/uploads/2019/09/Unclassified09.2019.pdf.

13. Tim Hains, "FLASHBACK, 2018: Joe Biden Brags at CFR Meeting About Withholding Aid to Ukraine to Force Firing of Prosecutor," Real Clear Politics, September 27, 2019, https://www.realclearpolitics.com/video/2019/09/27/flashback_2018_joe_biden_brags_at_cfr_meeting_about_withholding_aid_to_ukraine_to_force_firing_of_prosecutor.html.

14. Jake Gibson and Alex Pappas, "Source Says Whistleblower Didn't Have 'Firsthand Knowledge' of Trump call with Ukraine President," Fox News, September 23, 2019, https://www.foxnews.com/politics/source-says-whistleblower-didnt-have-firsthand-knowledge-of-trump-call-with-ukraine-president.

15. Ellie Bufkin, "Schiff Says His Summary of Trump's Ukraine Call Was 'at Least Part in Parody,'" *Washington Examiner*, September 26, 2019, https://www.washingtonexaminer.com/news/schiff-claims-his-summary-of-trumps-call-was-at-least-part-in-parody.

16. Rebecca Shabad, "Pelosi Says House Won't Hold Impeachment Vote 'at This Time,'" NBC News, October 15, 2020, https://www.nbcnews.com/politics/trump-impeachment-inquiry/pelosi-says-house-won-t-hold-vote-impeachment-time-n1066671.

17. Heather Caygle and Sarah Ferris, "'I'm Not Going to Take any Sh--': Nadler Girds for Battle," *Politico,* December 3, 2019, https://www.politico.com/news/2019/12/03/nadler-judiciary-impeachment-074985.

18. "Liberals Push to Impeach Bush," *Washington Times,* April 6, 2007, https://www.washingtontimes.com/news/2007/apr/6/20070406-124129-1462r/.

19. Isabel Vincent, "How Trump's Television City Started a Decades-Long Feud between Trump and Nadler," *New York Post,* July 27, 2019, https://nypost.com/2019/07/27/how-trumps-television-city-started-a-decades-long-feud-between-trump-and-nadler/.

20. Fred Kaplan, "Jerry's Revenge," *Slate*, December 3, 2019, https://slate.com/news-and-politics/2019/12/trump-nadler-new-york-real-estate-television-city.html.

21. Ibid.

22. Joseph Wulfsohn, "CNN Analyst: It's a 'Problem' for Dems That Impeachment Witnesses Never Met Trump," Fox News, November 13, 2019, https://www.foxnews.com/media/cnn-jeffrey-toobin-ambassador-bill-taylor-george-kent.

23. Norman Eisen and Noah Bookbinder, "Time for a Special Counsel in the Russiagate Scandal," *Politico,* March 3, 2020, https://www.politico.com/magazine/story/2017/03/donald-trump-russia-contacts-special-counsel-214859.

24. Daregh Gregorian, "Schiff Slams GOP Senators on Whistleblower Questions: 'Disgraceful,'" NBC News, January 30, 2020, https://www.nbcnews.com/politics/trump-impeachment-inquiry/schiff-slams-gop-senators-whistleblower-questions-disgraceful-n1126991.

25. Alexei Koseff and John Wildermuth, "Gov. Gavin Newsom Signs Bill Sending Mail Ballot to Every Active California Voter," June 18, 2020, https://www.sfchronicle.com/politics/article/Bill-to-send-a-mail-ballot-to-every-active-15349881.php.

26. President Donald Trump, interview on *The Savage Nation,* June 15, 2020.

27. Marshall Cohen, "Trump Spreads New Lies about Foreign-Backed Voter Fraud, Stoking Fears of a 'Rigged Election' This November," CNN, June 22, 2020, https://www.cnn.com/2020/06/22/politics/trump-voter-fraud-lies-fact-check/index.html.

28. "A Sampling of Election Fraud Cases from across the Country," Heritage Foundation, https://www.whitehouse.gov/sites/whitehouse.gov/files/docs/pacei-voterfraudcases.pdf.

29. J. Edward Moreno, "Here's Where Your State Stands on Mail-in Voting," *Hill*, June 9, 2020, https://thehill.com/homenews/state-watch/501577-heres-where-your-state-stands-on-mail-in-voting.

30. "Considerations for Election Polling Locations and Voters," Centers for Disease Control and Prevention, updated June 22, 2020, https://www.cdc.gov/coronavirus/2019-ncov/community/election-polling-locations.html.

CHAPTER 11: NEOCONS AND RINOS ARE STILL AMONG US

1. "Transcript of President Dwight D. Eisenhower's Farewell Address (1961)," Our Documents, https://www.ourdocuments.gov/doc. php?flash=false&doc=90&page=transcript.

2. https://twitter.com/ASavageNation/status/1273453028784259072?s=20.

3. Ryan Teague Beckwith, "Read Donald Trump's 'America First' Foreign Policy Speech," *Time,* April 27, 2016, https://time.com/4309786/read-donald-trumps-america-first-foreign-policy-speech/.

4. Nina Totenberg, "Supreme Court Rules for DREAMers, Against Trump," NPR, June 18, 2020, https://www.npr.org/2020/06/18/829858289/supreme-court-upholds-daca-in-blow-to-trump-administration.

5. Tala Hadavi, "Supreme Court ruling in Louisiana case sets back abortion foes' hopes of overturning Roe v. Wade," CNBC, July 4, 2020, https://www.cnbc.com/2020/07/04/supreme-court-decision-in-louisiana-case-sets-back-abortion-foes.html.

6. Veronica Stracqualursi, "The Prominent Former Military Leaders Who Have Criticized Trump's Actions over Protests," CNN, June 5, 2020, https://www.cnn.com/2020/06/05/politics/military-leaders-trump-floyd-protests/index.html.

7. Allan Smith, "Colin Powell Calls Trump a Liar, Says He Skirts the Constitution, Will Vote Biden," NBC News, June 7, 2020, https://www.nbcnews.com/politics/donald-trump/colin-powell-calls-trump-liar-says-he-skirts-constitution-will-n1227016.

8. Gregory Korte, Alan Gomez, and Kevin Johnson, "Trump Administration Struggles with Fate of 900 DREAMers Serving in the Military," *USA Today,* September 7, 2017, https://www.usatoday.com/story/news/politics/2017/09/07/trump-administration-struggles-fate-900-dreamers-serving-military/640637001/.

9. Gustavo López and Jens Manuel Krogstad, "Key Facts about Unauthorized Immigrants Enrolled in DACA," Pew Research Center, September 25, 2017, https://www.pewresearch.org/fact-tank/2017/09/25/key-facts-about-unauthorized-immigrants-enrolled-in-daca/.

10. David Nakamura, "How Many People Will Trump's DACA Rollback Affect? About 100,000 Fewer than Initially Reported," *Washington Post,* September 7, 2017, https://www.washingtonpost.com/news/post-politics/wp/2017/09/07/how-many-people-will-trumps-daca-rollback-affect-about-100000-fewer-than-initially-reported/.

11. "DHS Statement on Supreme Court Decision on DACA," Department of Homeland Security, June 18, 2020, https://www.dhs.gov/news/2020/06/18/dhs-statement-supreme-court-decision-daca.

12. Emily Cochrane and Aishvarya Kavi, "Romney Marches with Protesters in Washington," *New York Times,* June 7, 2020, https://www.nytimes.com/2020/06/07/us/politics/mitt-romney-george-floyd-protests.html.

13. James Walker, "Why Donald Trump's Approval Rating Is So High Among Republicans," *Newsweek,* June 17, 2020, https://www.newsweek.com/why-donald-trump-approval-rating-so-high-republicans-1511435.

14. Jacqueline Alemany with Brent D. Griffiths, "Power Up: Anti-Trump Republicans Are Now Getting Out the Vote for Joe Biden," *Washington Post,* June 26, 2020, https://www.washingtonpost.com/news/powerpost/paloma/powerup/2020/06/26/powerup-anti-trump-republicans-are-now-getting-out-the-vote-for-joe-biden/5ef4e32688e0fa7b44f67e16/.

15. Ibid.

CHAPTER 12: STARING INTO THE ABYSS

1. Fyodor Dostoevsky, *The Brothers Karamazov: A Novel in Four Parts with Epilogue*, translated and annotated by Richard Pevear and Larissa Volokhonsky (New York: Farrar, Straus & Giroux, 1990), p. 107.

2. "Black Lives Matter Group Storms Beverly Hills Residential Area: 'Eat The Rich!' 'Abolish Capitalism Now!," Daily Wire, June 27, 2020, https://www.dailywire.com/news/black-lives-matter-group-storms-beverley-hills-residential-area-eat-the-rich-abolish-capitalism-now.

3. "Beverly Hills Police Criticized for Arresting 28 Protesters," Spectrum News1, June 29, 2020, https://spectrumnews1.com/ca/la-west/public-safety/2020/06/29/beverly-hills-police-criticized-for-arresting-28-protesters.

4. Danielle Wallace, "Protesters Set Up Guillotine in Front of Jeff Bezos' DC Home: Reports," Fox News, June 29, 2020, https://www.foxnews.com/us/amazon-jeff-bezos-guillotine-dc-protests.

5. Maria Godoy, "Black Medicare Patients with COVID-19 Nearly 4 Times as Likely to End Up in Hospital," NPR, June 22, 2020, https://www.npr.org/sections/health-shots/2020/06/22/881886733/black-medicare-patients-with-covid-19-nearly-4-times-as-likely-to-end-up-in-hosp.

6. Jon Miltimore, "Blue States Have Been Hit Much Harder by COVID-19. Why?" Foundation for Economic Education, June 30, 2020, https://fee.org/articles/blue-states-have-been-hit-much-harder-by-covid-19-why/.

7. Edward Peter Stringham, "Again, What Were the Benefits of Locking Down?" American Institute for Economic Research, June 25, 2020, https://www.aier.org/article/again-what-were-the-benefits-of-locking-down/.

8. "Report: Nearly Half of All Coronavirus Deaths in US Occurred Inside Nursing Homes," Fox6 Now, June 28, 2020, https://fox6now.

com/2020/06/28/report-nearly-half-of-all-coronavirus-deaths-in-us-occurred-inside-nursing-homes/.

9. Ronn Blitzer, "Cuomo Dodges Repeated Questions on Whether New York Nursing Homes Are Safe," Fox News, June 28, 2020, https://www.foxnews.com/politics/cuomo-dodges-repeated-questions-on-whether-new-york-nursing-homes-are-safe.

10. Caroline Torie, "Michigan and Indiana Residents Ordered to Stay at Home for 2 Weeks to 'Flatten the Curve,'" WSBT22, March 23, 2020, https://wsbt.com/news/regional/michigan-and-indiana-residents-ordered-to-stay-at-home-for-2-weeks-to-flatten-the-curve.

11. Kai Kupferschmidt, "Study Claiming New Coronavirus Can Be Transmitted by People without Symptoms Was Flawed," *Science,* February 3, 2020, https://www.sciencemag.org/news/2020/02/paper-non-symptomatic-patient-transmitting-coronavirus-wrong?fbclid=IwAR3zwjnkT3K2YR4Jr4I4jL9r8SYyFwXrJyXyeThqOssZsCJlA8z0BDHc4K8.

12. "Quantifying SARS-CoV-2 Transmission Suggests Epidemic Control with Digital Contact Tracing," *Science,* May 8, 2020, https://science.sciencemag.org/content/368/6491/eabb6936.

13. Christianna Silva, "Parties—Not Protests—Are Causing Spikes in Coronavirus," NPR, June 24, 2020, https://www.npr.org/sections/coronavirus-live-updates/2020/06/24/883017035/what-contact-tracing-may-tell-about-cluster-spread-of-the-coronavirus.

14. "Daily Updates of Totals by Week and State," Centers for Disease Control and Prevention, https://www.cdc.gov/nchs/nvss/vsrr/covid19/index.htm.

15. Patrick J. Buchanan, "Are Uncivil Protests and Mob Violence Winning?," Patrick Buchanan official website, July 2, 2020, https://buchanan.org/blog/are-uncivil-protests-and-mob-violence-winning-138853.

16. Caleb Parke, "Outrage after California Bans Singing in Churches amid Coronavirus Pandemic," Fox News, July 6, 2020, https://www.foxnews.com/us/california-singing-ban-church-coronavirus-restriction.

17. Marlei Martinez, "California Pastor: COVID-19 Church Singing Ban 'Infringes on Religious Rights," KCRA 3, July 3, 2020, https://www.kcra.com/article/california-pastor-covid-19-church-singing-ban-infringes-on-religious-rights/33146995.

18. Post Editorial Board, "Mayor de Blasio, Do Something about the Deaths in Our Streets," *New York Post,* July 6, 2020, https://nypost.com/2020/07/06/mayor-de-blasio-do-something-about-the-deaths-in-our-streets/.

19. Tom Bawden, "It's Time to Decolonise Botanical Collections, Says Kew Gardens Director," I News, June 21, 2020, https://inews.co.uk/news/

environment/time-to-decolonise-botanical-collections-kew-gardens-director-alexandre-antonelli-452109.

20. Theresa Seiger, "Frederick Douglass Statue Torn from Base on Anniversary of Famous Speech," Fox 13, July 6, 2020, https://www.fox13memphis.com/news/trending/frederick-douglass-statue-torn-base-anniversary-famous-speech/4BZNAJEKGREXFCYXYSIE7NJNRY/.

21. Ian Shapira, "For 200 Years, the Insurrection Act Has Given Presidents the Power to Deploy the Military to Quell Unrest," *Washington Post,* June 3, 2020, https://www.washingtonpost.com/history/2020/06/03/insurrection-act-trump-history/.